Hamlet

Hamlet

Essays from the annual Loughborough Shakespeare Conference

edited by
Ian Clarke

LTT
Loughborough Theatre Texts
Loughborough

First published in 1994 by
Loughborough Theatre Texts
Department of English and Drama
Loughborough University
Loughborough
LE11 3TU

Reprinted 1996
Reprinted 1999

Printed by
Audio-Visual Services
Loughborough University

British Library Cataloguing-in-Publication Data is
available from the British Library

ISBN 1-898726-01-9

Contents

*Illustrations between pages 56 and 58 are
by Christine White*

Cover design by Alison Maclaurin

Acknowledgements

Thanks are due to the staff and students of the Department of English and Drama who have made the 1999 Annual Shakespeare Conference that accompanies this book:

Vanessa Adlard, Hannah Brewer, Anne Courtenay-Smith, Bethany Darbyshire, Ruth Falconbridge, Emma Goodridge, Viv Green, Rachel Halcrow, David Hill, Sarah Hulme, Phillipa Knapp, Alison Maclaurin, Marianna Maniatakis, Audrey Mifsud, Robin Nelson, Caroline Payne, Jessica Rees, Clare Saunders, Natalie Spear, Rachel White, Laura Whyman, Shelley Wilson, Suzanne Wynne.

Preface

This book is designed to be of use to A-level and undergraduate students. It is published in association with the nineteenth annual Shakespeare Conference mounted by the Department of English and Drama at Loughborough University. At the Conference, A-level students from across the East Midlands will attend practical presentations and lectures, and participate in group discussions on *Hamlet*. The play, as is customary, has been chosen by local schools and colleges; staff and students in the Department at Loughborough write, rehearse, and prepare materials for presentation.

The Conference and this volume, then, are first of all designed to help students pass examinations. But both are also in some degree openly designed to make an intervention. Many students at A-level or its equivalent will go on to study Drama or Literature in higher education. The process of sitting for school and college examinations is a proper end in itself, but can also be a preparation for further work. We aim to nudge this in appropriate directions.

Put bluntly—and though we recognise a wide variety of teaching and learning practices—we would encourage English Literature A-level study to attend more to the theatrical nature of dramatic texts, and Theatre Studies A-level students to attend more both to the cultural contexts of dramatic writing, and to the way in which dramatic scripts inscribe a wide variety of relations between both performer and role and spectacle and audience. Each essay in this volume attends in some way to this need.

Hamlet and the Court

BILL OVERTON

Anyone coming to study Shakespeare for the first time is likely to meet, first of all, a text. This will be laid out in a special way, not as a story but as dialogue and stage directions - though often with notes as well. Technically, it is a dramatic text, but, even though it is dramatic, written for the stage, it is easily read as if it were a novel. One chief aim of the Shakespeare Conference is to encourage a different kind of reading. It is to turn, or return, the dramatic text into a theatrical text. Such a text is to be read not by looking at words on a page, but by witnessing, on a stage in front of you, speech, action and various effects. This paper has been written with the same aim in view, even though, unlike two other papers in the book, it is not linked with a stage presentation. For this reason much of the discussion is keyed to passages of the play approached not only as text, but as theatre.

One of the problems in developing such an approach is that it can be difficult to get an idea from the text of the kind of world to be shown onstage. I want to begin, therefore, by setting up an idea of the kind of world dramatised, or theatricalised, in *Hamlet*. This is partly to help give some sense of how the play might look onstage. Mostly, however, it is because I think that knowing something about the social world implied by the play is an important part of understanding it.

The original story of *Hamlet* is set in a harsh Viking world close in many ways to that of *Macbeth*. In adapting that story for the stage, Shakespeare brought it up to date in a way which must have been striking for the play's first audiences. The court in which Claudius operates is like that of the Tudors or, a few years after the play's first performances, James I, and there were others like it elsewhere in Europe. It is possible to get some idea of it from two works written earlier in the sixteenth century. One, Castiglione's *Book of the Courtier* (published in 1561 in a translation by Sir Thomas Hoby), gives an idealised account of courtly behaviour in the Italian dukedom of Urbino. People in Castiglione's court spend their time in such cultivated pursuits as chivalric swordplay, music, poetry, philosophical discussion and Platonic love. The other book, Machiavelli's *The Prince*, is just the opposite. This is a book about how to use power, and especially about how to keep it. Machiavelli takes it for granted that power is a thing of this world, not of an ideal one. So, for him, ends justify means, and the key end of maintaining power may require the ruler to deceive, manipulate, or eliminate those who stand in his way. Although *The Prince* did not appear in English until 1640, it caused moral shockwaves across Europe, and the idea of Machiavelli which resulted is still fixed in our language. To be Machiavellian is, at the least, to stop at nothing in pursuit of one's aims. At the time *Hamlet* was first performed, it was more likely to suggest gratuitous evil - crime and treachery for their own sake.

Castiglione and Machiavelli created opposite images of what courtly life might be like. Both kinds of image are presented at various times in *Hamlet*, and I suggest that, by putting these together, it is possible to form a sense of the social world of the play. One example is the sequence, often cut in productions, in which Claudius, egging Laertes on to revenge, paints a striking picture of courtly rivalry. He describes the Norman Lamord, whose skill on horseback 'Had witchcraft in't' (4.7.84), and whom Laertes calls 'the brooch indeed / And gem of all the nation' (4.7.92-3). Then he goes on to tell how Lamord made Hamlet jealous by praising Laertes's skill at swordplay. Claudius is, of course, as often, lying; but what he is trying to do is to turn accomplishments worthy of Castiglione's court into a trap worthy of a Machiavellian. As he and Laertes go on to frame their triple play of duel, venom and poison, the ideal portrait of the courtier suddenly gives way to the reality. Claudius has little in him of Castiglione's courtier, but everything that Shakespeare's contemporaries feared and hated in their idea of Machiavelli.

Another sequence, a little later in the play and again often cut in production, makes the same point in a different way. This is the sequence in which Osric carries Laertes's challenge to Hamlet. Osric is both a decadent perversion of Castiglione's ideals and an instrument of the king's Machiavellianism. It is a common mistake to play him for laughs, in a sideshow for Hamlet to score satirical points off a fop. The trouble is that Osric seems hardly bothered by Hamlet's wit. He ignores the gibes and keeps on till he has delivered his message, not giving up a bit of his affected eloquence or etiquette. A fop Osric certainly is, but in this context his assurance is sinister. In production, this absurd encounter is most effective when it produces tension, not comic relief. It is a restatement, just before the play's climax, of its basic opposition. Hamlet, alone except for his one friend Horatio, faces the corrupt and powerful court which will kill him even as he takes revenge.

Hamlet versus the court, Castiglione versus Machiavelli: here are two rough-and-ready contrasts to open up the play. But there is also a further contrast, and, more problematic, a fundamental absence. The third contrast comes from the frame in which Shakespeare enclosed his action. In the opening scene Horatio paints a stirring picture of old Hamlet as a hero-king who 'smote the sledded Polacks on the ice' (1.1.66), and killed his challenger in single combat. The next scene opens on the very different world of Claudius and his court. This transition mirrors what Shakespeare had done to his plot, for he had brought an archaic Viking tale disturbingly into the present. It also marks out a contemporary context of social and political change. Shakespeare wrote Hamlet shortly after the ill-fated Essex rebellion, and the accession of James I gave only a temporary solution to a problem which became civil war under the very next king. The links between the play and contemporary English history are complex and indirect, but the difference between old Hamlet and Claudius reflects a vision of a feudal ethos giving way to one based on calculation and expediency. Claudius's court represents a new political reality. Shakespeare had shown that reality arriving in his History plays, and he was to dramatise a similar conflict in *Troilus and Cressida*, the tragedy he wrote next. His success in presenting it in *Hamlet* owes a lot to what he had learned in the Histories, especially to his skill at creating a convincing social world and a sense of historical perspective. The perspective is one of loss and tragic irony. Hamlet, born the day his father killed old Fortinbras, is to be succeeded by young Fortinbras at the end.

I mentioned that there is also a fundamental absence in the social world of this play, and it should be obvious: this is a court without women. Literally, performances of *Hamlet* until after the Restoration lacked women, as women were not allowed to act on the public stage. But I think that the very limited characterisation given to Gertrude and Ophelia makes the same point figuratively valid too. Playing Gertrude must be a thankless task, as the play requires her to be stupid. Playing Ophelia cannot be much better, unless (if the performer can stand it) as a sentimentalised victim, most of all in the mad sequence of Act 4 Scene 5. These are revealing deficiencies, and not only in light of the important roles women have to play in Castiglione's *Book of the Courtier*. Women were scarcely absent from the English court; at the time the play was first performed, one happened to be queen. Among Shakespeare's tragedies *Hamlet* is anything but the only one to give sharply restricted roles to women. Though that is a question beyond my scope in the present paper,[1] this fact about the play brings its social world much closer to the world described by Machiavelli, in which women are also almost wholly lacking.

That world is first presented in the council scene of Act 1. The scene needs to be watched without bias if what it has to show is to be picked up clearly, and this means holding back any presuppositions that may have come from study or hearsay. Looked at this way, Claudius may at first come off impressively enough and it is Hamlet who may seem out of place. He has not been mentioned till the end of the previous scene, he does not speak until well into this one, and his behaviour seems awkward and sulky. Claudius is a good politician, if not a man of action like his brother. Where old Hamlet had put himself on the line, fighting old Fortinbras to the death, Claudius gets young Fortinbras stopped by a diplomatic message. He has already boldly confronted any doubts that may linger over his marriage. Finally he moves to private business, paying generous tribute to Polonius and his son, and handling Hamlet with apparent tolerance and discretion.

This at least is probably how the court sees the occasion, but the signs to the audience are more ambiguous. Claudius is effective but suspiciously slick. Nowhere is he more ingratiating than when he favours Laertes; and his motive is a snub to Hamlet who has not yet spoken but cannot be showing approval for what he is seeing. Yet Claudius allows his nephew to appear the aggressor. Hamlet's opening words, 'A little more than kin, and less than kind' (1.2.65), do not have to be spoken aside, despite what nearly all the editions say.[2] The point is that Claudius does not acknowledge them. His tactic is to deny the reality of Hamlet's feelings. He acts the wise uncle in his sermon on grief, but the masterstroke of his policy is to seal Hamlet's enforced stay by naming him heir apparent. His formal language emphasises his power and presents the announcement as a ceremony. But phrases such as 'a loving and a fair reply' (121) and 'This gentle and unforced accord' (123) are clearly disinformation. If Hamlet plays along, all well and good; if not, he has already been defined as rebellious and ungrateful.

There can be few more powerful motivations in drama than that for Hamlet's first soliloquy. Utterly isolated, aware that something is desperately wrong, and now put in check by Claudius, he breaks out into violent, even at times hardly articulate protest. This is the response of one who cannot be denoted truly by the conventionality of the court. What is at issue here is a question of values. For Hamlet, Claudius has literally adulterated the kingdom. It is not only that the incestuous marriage betrays a hero's memory, but that it has infected the state with artifice and duplicity. The last words of the soliloquy, 'But break, my heart, for I must hold my tongue' (1.2.159), show Hamlet's need to be on guard. He must now suspect everyone.

But the entry of Horatio and the others allows Hamlet's values a positive statement. When he recognises his friends, he gives a warm, wholehearted welcome. Hamlet, though a prince, refuses to let Horatio call himself his servant and insists: 'I'll change that name with you' (163). He won't allow Horatio to do himself down with the phrase 'A truant disposition' (169), and he speaks his mind to his friend. Paying tribute to his father, he shows his essential priorities. To Horatio's 'a [i.e. he] was a goodly king', he replies, 'A was a man' (186-7); for Hamlet it is the example of male value that matters, not the rank. After he listens to the account of the Ghost's appearance, there is a similar touch when he insists, as on meeting Horatio, not on the duty he is owed as a prince but on the mutual good feeling of companions (1.2.252-3). When they leave the stage, the exposition to the tragedy is complete. The scene has unfolded through three main movements which define the world of the play. There is the court, and the mind of Hamlet; but also the chance, hemmed in though it is, of freedom and equality between male friends.

The next scene moves back to the ways of the court. Hamlet has just affirmed the values of friendship and masculine worth, irrespective of rank; now Laertes tells Ophelia that the prince's rank makes him fickle and dangerous. Laertes's affectionate tone is belied by the doubts he casts on his sister's chastity - in that society, her one possible source of good social standing. Polonius, though her father, is harsher and grosser. But it is unlikely that either's reason for warning her is really a moral one. Instead, Hamlet is not much of a prospect if he is going to fall out with the king. The start of Act 2 shows further how the suspicion and scheming of the court have spread into the family. Having given his son a fatherly farewell, and a set of worldly maxims to digest, Polonius falsifies both by briefing an informer to follow him. Before Polonius can offer himself as a spy on Hamlet, with Ophelia as bait, his king is up to similar tricks. As Polonius is to Reynaldo, so is Claudius to Rosencrantz and Guildenstern: a parallel implied by the juxtaposition of the two scenes. Similarly, there is a contrast with Hamlet's treatment of the new arrivals. Meeting Rosencrantz and Guildenstern, his welcome is as warm as theirs is sycophantic, yet he does not immediately take offence. While they answer him with evasions, he appeals to them in the name of friendship. When they try to put words into his mouth, probing what they suppose to be his ambition, he cuts short the sophisticated backchat with the ironic suggestion that it is strictly for the court, not suitable for a talk between friends. By the end of the sequence they have enlisted themselves once and for all on the court's side against him. Repeating his welcome sardonically, he practically tells them so. If Rosencrantz and Guildenstern are pawns in the power game, the trouble is that they are so willing. They are complicated by none of the sense Tom Stoppard gives them, in his play *Rosencrantz and Guildenstern Are Dead*, of the absurdity of existence. Rather it is Hamlet who expresses such a sense in his speech on the dignity and emptiness of man. He opens up a perspective on life which means nothing to them. Their response is a deaf or at best a facetious ear, followed by a lucky diversion to the players.

This same contrast between idealism and corruption is focused again in the opening scene of Act 3, but this time more sharply. First, there is just embarrassment. Rosencrantz and Guildenstern have made so little of Hamlet that their report is almost comically shuffling and contradictory. Much more surprising is Claudius's anguished aside when, ironically, Polonius's hollow moralising strikes home. Shakespeare does not deny humanity to his villains; the Machiavellian has moral problems too. But these will stop Claudius no more than they bother Polonius, and it is the effects of their practices on Hamlet and Ophelia which disturb most. The sequence in which Hamlet repudiates Ophelia is one of the most painful and difficult in the play. One common way of explaining it is the suggestion that Hamlet notices he is being spied on and assumes that Ophelia is part of a conspiracy against him.[3] This seems to make sense, but two facts disqualify it. First, Elizabethan dramatic convention always required that a person aware of being spied on should indicate that awareness clearly.[4] Hamlet does not do this. Second, there's the question of what role Ophelia plays. The problem here, as I suggested earlier, is that the role is under-written. In other words, there are not enough clues in the text to define what her role is in relation to Hamlet and his enemies, and I find it difficult not to suppose that she is little more than a dramatic convenience. What I will offer is one possible reading of the lines given, as a way of producing the character onstage. This reading is in keeping with what I take to be the emphases of the play, although, as I have said, I think that these themselves should be treated critically.

The first question is why Hamlet fails to see Ophelia when he enters. As her father has instructed her to walk to and fro so that Hamlet may meet her, one plausible explanation is that she chooses differently. It is Hamlet who speaks first when he sees her, and, significantly, she is praying. This suggests reluctance, not complicity with her father's conspiracy. When she returns the gifts, Ophelia obeys Polonius's order to end the relationship; but she says nothing to invite any giveaway responses which Claudius and Polonius might overhear. She is caught in what psychologists call a double bind. Loving Hamlet, she has been told not to see him. Now this command has been reversed, but in a scheme which is kept obscure to her and which she could hardly approve. She cannot show him affection because she is acting under constraint. Yet because she behaves, as she must, so stiffly, she is attacked and denied his love. From Hamlet's point of view, Ophelia is betraying him. He knows nothing of the lies she has been told or of the constraints that bind her. But there are other reasons why he rounds on her so violently. The most obvious is the parallel he sees with his mother. What seems to be treachery from Ophelia compounds his sense of Gertrude's betrayal and marks all women as tainted.[5]

Secondly, Hamlet's violence is partly his antic disposition. When he acts the madman, he is both confusing his enemies and giving himself space for verbal retaliation. That is why he bewilders Ophelia with the same sudden unsettling questions and enigmas which he puts to Polonius. Yet he is not only retaliating. The antic disposition is also a safe if provocative outlet for disgust and frustration. But, although Ophelia occasions his outburst, she is not its only target. Hamlet also accuses, by implication, Gertrude, Polonius, and Claudius; and, directly, himself. He too is marked by a guilt which he knows and feels even as he rejects Ophelia. So the third explanation of his behaviour is a kind of intensity which compels him to take his experience at full pressure. This powerful responsiveness is the source of his volatility, and it has the defects of its merits. The same energy that supplies Hamlet's sharp, clear sense of values, his capacity for radical questions, can also boil over into intolerance. But, again, Ophelia only catches part of this. For instead of blaming him for his violence, or collapsing under it, she can only understand him as mad. The sequence in which Hamlet treats her worst ends in her tribute to the perfect courtier he had been.

What should not be lost on the audience is how the schemes of another kind of courtier have led to their division. Again, a theatrical reading of the text is available which does not require Ophelia to have been complicit. For example, Polonius's advice that she need not repeat what Hamlet has said can be read to suggest that she does not know about the eavesdropping. Similarly, Hamlet's question 'Where's your father?' (3.1.130-1) has the effect of raising the dramatic temperature and of reminding the audience of the spies; it does not have to imply that he knows he is being spied on, and all the other evidence tells against this. Instead, the impact of the sequence comes from two juxtapositions which frame it. It begins and ends with soliloquies which show up the eavesdroppers' meanness and duplicity. In this Machiavellian context, Ophelia's tribute to Hamlet evokes an ideal courtier in terms that recall Castiglione. And his own most famous speech justifies the tribute by opening up questions which transcend those of spying and intrigue. While king and minister scheme to counteract him, he meditates on the ends of action; and he is to face as an obstacle to action the conscience which nags Claudius too late.

The issue of 'To be, or not to be' is whether life is worth living when it seems a choice between suffering in silence, and action which can only prove self-destructive. It is a question to which Hamlet's case allows no acceptable answer, and he leaves it unresolved. Nevertheless his soliloquy lights up what it means to live and to act in the world - especially a court, where questions of power over others are at issue. The nettle to be grasped is that deciding whether to live or to die entails both penalties and responsibilities. These will come home to Hamlet in the second half of the play. But what the soliloquy also expresses is a vivid, flesh-and-blood sense of what life can be like for ordinary men, who bear 'Th'oppressor's wrong, the proud man's contumely' and 'grunt and sweat under a weary life' (3.1.71, 77). I use the word 'men' deliberately because neither the play, nor Hamlet's own behaviour, displays the same insight into the lives of women. Nevertheless, it takes great sympathy and imagination for a prince to picture what King Lear and Gloucester learn only after themselves undergoing the sufferings of the poor; and for a moment it is possible to glimpse what Hamlet might be like as king.

Hamlet's most famous soliloquy forms a kind of thinking space before he intervenes against Claudius. The rest of the play shows both the nature of his action and its effects. In more ways than one, the play within the play is the catalyst, setting off a train of powerful ironies. First, Hamlet confirms that Claudius is guilty at the cost of laying himself open to public suspicion. Second, the play is so successful in stirring up the king's guilt that Hamlet is led to refuse his only chance of killing Claudius safely. In his speech beginning 'Now might I do it pat' (3.3.73ff.), Hamlet means exactly what he says. He really does want ultimate revenge, and he passes up the opportunity because he believes that someone who dies praying will end up in paradise, even if he is a murderer. It is often suggested that in his speech Hamlet is just rationalising an inability to act, and such a view is attractive because his words are so shocking. But it does not match either his bloodthirsty determination at the end of the previous scene ('Now could I drink hot blood', 3.2.381), or his killing of Polonius in the one after.

What has to be recognised is that after 'To be, or not to be' Hamlet's thinking narrows - and that this is the result of a choice to fight the king's Machiavellianism with its own weapons. The Ghost has urged Hamlet, 'Taint not thy mind' (1.5.85), but this is precisely what he cannot avoid in embracing the role of revenger. Shakespeare presses the lesson home through the killing of Polonius. Not only is this wrong in itself, despite the crime of spying. It also turns Hamlet into an object of revenge, and unhinges Ophelia's sanity. In other words, the play puts in question the whole idea of revenge. This is easy to see when Laertes says he would cut Hamlet's throat in church to avenge his father and Claudius smoothly replies: 'No place indeed should murder sanctuarize; / Revenge should have no bounds' (4.7.126-7). It is a chilling moment, yet Hamlet has acted on just the same principle in resolving to terminate Claudius with extremer prejudice. So there arises a very difficult problem of response - not so much to the character as to the kinds of principle on which he will act. What kind of a hero is Hamlet when he commits himself, in a Machiavellian court, to such appallingly ultimate vengeance?

There are several ways to answer this question, but it is more important to recognise what makes it necessary to ask it. Essentially, *Hamlet* is a play designed to put audiences on the spot. It forces questions about political and personal morality by confronting audiences with intractable dilemmas. Here, one possible reply is that Hamlet is right to act against Claudius as a king who got his throne by murder. In this way Hamlet's fault would be his commitment to a personal revenge, and its wrongness would be shown first by his speech in the prayer scene, and then in action when he kills Polonius and sets off another cycle of suffering and vengeance. But such a view is not acceptable without several qualifications. One is that the quality of Hamlet's thought and feeling is likely to engage sympathy, and to hold it even when the king's struggle with his conscience pulls the other way. Another is his potential as prince and as man. Only Hamlet can imagine what life is like for ordinary men, as he does in his central soliloquy; although it is also only Hamlet who can imagine an ultimate revenge. This means that one element in his tragedy is the moral and spiritual guilt he takes on in becoming a revenger. But it also points to the third qualification, which is that the task he is called on to perform offers no satisfactory solution. It is all very well to argue that Hamlet should challenge Claudius as king. But the king enjoys the confidence of his court, and Hamlet cannot prove he is guilty.

The play's other two revenge actions set Hamlet's problem in relief. If he is to be accused of delay, or of thinking too precisely on the event, it has to be asked whether the brash brutality and treachery of Laertes is really preferable. The second alternative seems no better. Fortinbras never avenges his father's death because Claudius stops him by diplomacy. Instead he amuses himself with his Polish exploit till he finds the throne of Denmark luckily vacant. The depth of

Hamlet's impasse can be gauged from his final soliloquy, 'How all occasions do inform against me' (4.4.32ff.), called out of him by the sight of Fortinbras and his army. Hamlet finds in Fortinbras a renewed example and incentive for revenge. Yet the terms in which he casts the lesson are contradictory. It is wrong for him to find a motive in such humanly wasteful absurdity. The plainspoken Captain tells him the expedition is pointless, and he himself scorns it as a cancer in the body politic, fed by 'a fantasy and trick of fame' (4.4.61). Why then should it affect him? The answer must lie in his frustration, sent off unsuccessful to England. Yet the speech also throws a different light on his difficulties. It begins by asking a fundamental question of the play, and of Shakespeare's tragedies: 'What is a man?' (4.4.33). The question looks back to Hamlet's meditation on man in his talk with Rosencrantz and Guildenstern, and the definition he proposes looks back further still, to the first soliloquy. What distinguishes a man (or, it might be added, a woman) is 'godlike reason' (4.4.38), the ability to think and speak. It is this ability in which Hamlet is so exceptional, yet the speech shows him torturing himself with an unreasonable example and rushing to the conclusion that from now on his thoughts must 'be bloody or be nothing worth' (4.4.66). As before, it is his own standards of humanity that Hamlet is brought to affront. The next scene shows where such thoughts may lead, when Ophelia enters insane.

There is a sense in which *Hamlet* is a peculiarly unfair play. It sets impossible problems for its hero, and it wrong-foots the audience persistently. Perhaps, then, it is only right that Shakespeare should give Hamlet a break in his adventure with the pirates. If the dramatist here seems to play God, he is at least in accord with the philosophy implied by his play. Hamlet's own words best express this when, in the lull before the climax, he tells Horatio: 'There is special providence in the fall of a sparrow', and 'The readiness is all' (5.2.215-16, 218). Yet the crucial point about the play's ending is that Claudius brings his downfall on himself. The triple villainy of sword, venom, and poison comes home to him, his instrument Laertes, and his Queen. It also gives Hamlet the chance both to expiate his killing of Polonius and to kill the king without taint.

Like the council sequence in Act 1, and the play scene in Act 3, the finale presents the court in full ceremony. The ceremony is to mask Claudius's murderous scheme, but it is placed in a still more revealing light by the episodes that introduce it. The last of these is the sequence already discussed involving Osric. But first comes the graveyard scene. The Gravedigger and his companion are the play's only spokesmen for a society beyond the court. They know that Ophelia would never have been buried as a Christian had she not been a lady, and their blunt commonsense puts an alternative view to the court's. Literally, they bring courtly sophistication down to earth: which is where even the finest lady or gentleman comes from, and where she or he will go. Part of this message Hamlet can echo, as he draws all his examples of mortality from types to be found in the court. But Hamlet also gets a lesson himself. His wit and eloquence meet their match in the Gravedigger's matter-of-factness, as Hamlet moves from meditating on a skull to the shock of discovering whose it is, and then of whom the grave is being dug for.

The Gravedigger offers another perspective to set against these rebukes to Hamlet's complacency. This has to do with the historical cycle behind the play which I mentioned earlier in this paper, and with its political implications. He recalls that Hamlet was born on the day his father killed old Fortinbras; and Hamlet is to die with the wish that young Fortinbras succeed him. In other words, a story which began in feudal single combat ends in a duel whose hallmark is courtly villainy. Followed as it is by an adventurer's succession, this is deeply ironic. Further, Hamlet and Fortinbras get each other wrong, but in opposite ways. Hamlet asks that Fortinbras succeed him because he believes him to be 'a delicate and tender prince' (4.4.48) whose heroic enterprise has shamed him. But this view tells more about Hamlet himself than it does about Fortinbras, whose qualities are more aptly defined by his Polish campaign and by Horatio at the beginning of the play. Fortinbras as king of Denmark is probably better than Claudius, but not much. The point is what has been lost in Hamlet, and Hamlet's qualities are defined for the audience partly by what he sees in others: in his father and in Horatio, as well as in Fortinbras. They are travestied by the tribute Fortinbras gives him, which defines the latter's own nature instead. Fortinbras conveys only part of Hamlet's value in stating: 'For he was likely, had he been put on, / To have prov'd most royal' (5.2.402-3), and in giving him a soldier's funeral. Hamlet has been put to the test, and, though he has not avoided all the taints of the court, he has proved something better than royal. In the final scene he shows he can live up to the ideals he sees in others, but he has also demonstrated other qualities. Chief among these are his ability to ask basic questions about life, and his generosity to his friends. Earlier in the play, Polonius says he will treat the players as they deserve and Hamlet replies: 'Use every man after his desert, and who shall scape whipping?' (2.2.524-5). It is as if knowledge of human corruption makes generosity necessary: this reply alone could define Hamlet's value.

If that value suffers in the course of the action, this is the price of acting in a Machiavellian society. Hamlet's sentence on Rosencrantz and Guildenstern draws a raised eyebrow even from Horatio, and it is not only to gather the threads of the plot that their deaths are announced at the end. Yet, in Hamlet's ability to imagine what a man might be, and what life is like for those less privileged, Shakespeare illustrates a potential which the political structure shown in the play could hardly accommodate. Hamlet's quality as a prince reaches beyond what was possible not only to Machiavelli's court, but also to Castiglione's.

The view of the play I have given has been deliberately Hamlet-centred, because that is the response I believe it invites. But it is always possible to refuse or to renegotiate invitations, and I want to end by emphasising again what the play leaves out. This is the importance of women, as realised dramatic figures and in ways other than, here, as a sensual dupe or a fetishised victim. In order to explore some of the implications of the severely limited roles women have in the play, it would be worth imagining, say, Ophelia browbeating Hamlet as he browbeats her in Act 3 Scene 1, or Gertrude recoiling in aversion from men, like her son from sex, once she realises how appallingly they have treated her. The result of such thinking might not be Shakespeare as currently received, but that does not disqualify it. It might lead to fuller understanding of what is and is not allowed to be at issue in *Hamlet*, and what might further be at issue as the play continues in production and the syllabus.

1 See, for instance, French (1982).

2 The Arden edition is an exception, but, for instance, both the Penguin edition (Spencer, 1980) and the more recent New Cambridge edition (Edwards, 1985) make the speech an aside. The first editor to do so was Lewis Theobald in 1740.

3 J. Dover Wilson contributed most to the theory that Hamlet knows he is being spied on. See his edition of the play (1934) and *What Happens in 'Hamlet'*. The stage business of having Hamlet notice an incautious movement from one of the spies (usually Polonius) goes back to the early nineteenth century.

4 See the discussion by Jenkins (1982), especially pp. 496-7.

5 I leave it open to discussion whether this hysterical attribution of sexual taint to women is to be understood as Hamlet's response, as an assumption behind the play, or as a wider cultural prejudice.

'To be, or not to be' - what are the questions?

MICK WALLIS

About midway through the play, the hero comes to the front of the stage and talks to himself. We overhear him thinking through some important questions about life. The big problem, however, is in deciding just what his problem is. The problem is so difficult that hundreds of thousands of words have been written since, trying to establish the facts of the matter.

One of the chief problems of interpretation is this: Is Hamlet directly contemplating suicide, asking himself whether or not he should continue living ('to be')? Or is he rather challenging himself with a different, more general proposition, that in order really to live, one must act in the world, not just exist ('to be, one must do')?[1]

So much is written because the play *Hamlet* has become an important text in our culture. Its importance is partly tied up with the general notion of Shakespeare's special genius, his almost mythic status that persists still. I don't want to indulge here in the easy game of Shakespeare-bashing. I think that this particular play - like several but not all done by this actor-writer from the petty Warwickshire gentry - is not only brilliantly crafted, but is also (as a consequence) deeply engaging, both intellectually and at times emotionally.[2]

However, I do want to establish some sort of distance on both Shakespeare and his hero. Restoration and eighteenth-century playwrights had considered Shakespeare too disorderly: he mixed up different sorts of speech and action; his plays combined tragedy and comedy, high drama and low; they bristled with ugly phrases and raw emotion; they employed crazy time-schemes; they lacked all sorts of decorum, of measure. So Restoration writers 'corrected' Shakespeare's texts for performance, to 'civilise', to 'modernise', them.[3]

The construction of Shakespeare as the nation's (or the world's) supreme artist, the claim that he is of timeless significance, began to emerge with especial strength around 1800, and it is interesting to note that a key text in this revaluation was *Hamlet*. It has been well established that this new construction of Shakespeare was promoted especially by the Romantics in England and Germany.

Most generations of artists also act as critics: they revalue tradition in order to claim a position from which to speak, from which to make significant utterance - to make new art. An important part of the self-definition of the Romantics was a reaction against what they felt were the restrictions of decorum. Shakespeare was to be valued precisely *because* of his relative wildness. The extremes of emotion, the varieties of discourse, the complexity of action, the roller-coaster feel of his tragedies, in an important way rhymed with a feeling that radical change was now needed in political and social life in general. Such general feelings had found political expression in France in 1789, the year of the Revolution, and they remained current in much of the rest of Europe. Coupled with this radical disaffection was a stress on the ability of the individual imagination to break free from constraint, from the set rules of doing things and of seeing the world. The authentic individual - especially the artist - was seen as one who stood apart from the world, and imagined things otherwise. But the corollary of this was another feeling: of solitude. Standing apart is a way of claiming independence and a new vision. But it can also be lonely. Several of the Romantics in fact actively promoted this sense of martyrdom, of the lonely artist with access to a new vision, but misunderstood by the world, or unheard.

It is no surprise, then, that *Hamlet* became valued so highly by this generation of (mainly male) writers. Here was a potential rebel, one who stood apart from a corrupt order, and yet who was unable despite himself to act (to do, to be) in a significant way. Peter Womack has pointed out that several writers modelled themselves on Hamlet - or a Hamlet constructed out of the materials Shakespeare's play provided them with.[4]

It is as if, for that generation of writers, Hamlet spoke directly to them. And this sense of immediacy is tied up with a sense of Shakespeare's ability to speak directly to the reader (or the hearer) of his plays. The point of his plays, according to this mind-set, is his genius; they give us access to his great powers of understanding. Art, for the Romantics, rises above rules and above time. And Shakespeare, for many of them, was an heroic example of this ability.

One of the problems of the sort of reading outlined above is that it actually obscures Shakespeare's skill and importance. It would of course be fruitless to maintain an argument with artists and critics who have been dead for more than a century. But the fact is that the emphasis on Shakespeare's 'mind' and the 'mind' of his heroes has persisted very strongly since. Part of this is to do with how we (or they, if you don't feel part of it) as a nation have since used Shakespeare as an icon, a special marker for value: the Shakespeare of roast beef, Merrie England and Good Queen Bess. The 'new' Shakespeare soon became tamed, put to other, less radical, uses. But part of it is also due to Shakespeare's brilliance in developing one particular sort of dramatic writing.

Shakespeare himself lived in a time of deep and rapid change - economic, social and political. Such times are ones in which basic values get thought about deeply. They are times, usually too, of deep artistic innovation. In an earlier essay I sketched out the shape of that change, from a supposedly stable and timeless feudal system of production, of politics and of living, to what is basically the foundation of our modern way of living. Recent criticism of Renaissance plays has offered arguments around a basic observation: that Shakespeare and his contemporaries found ways of putting on stage a new feeling about the person, about the individual human being.[5]

One of the extraordinary things about the Hamlet soliloquy - and other speeches like it - is the way it produces the feeling of a depth of human personality that is in some way, and an important way, unknowable. In a play of just some twenty or thirty years previously, a protagonist might also appear on stage and speak alone. He might wrestle with his soul, address his conscience, report on his need for grace and the temptation of the devil. There is in fact a speech not unlike this in *Hamlet* itself. Look at Claudius's speech, 'O, my offence is rank, it smells to heaven' (3.3.36ff). In many ways it is, for Shakespeare's time, 'conventional', written to an old formula. He speaks of his guilt; says what heavenly mercy means, what power it has; reflects that he cannot truly pray for forgiveness while he still enjoys the fruits of his wrongdoing; contrasts heavenly justice with the 'corrupted currents of this world' (57); and suffers before our eyes as he tries to pray, but cannot.[6]

The speech is something like a moral commentary. Claudius is here produced almost like a picture of the wages of sin, the inevitable result of ambition. We know all we need to know about him. There is nothing difficult about the speech. It is as if the character were saying to the audience, 'Look at me, this is where wrongdoing gets you'.

There are two very obvious models for this sort of writing. One is the Medieval morality play such as *Everyman* (ca 1490), in which a protagonist taken to stand for humanity in general, a typical human being, has to decide whether to follow God's law and be saved, or to follow his own appetites and go to Hell.[7] Everyman and characters like him speak in much the confessional way that Claudius does here. And the manner of speaking, while it is in one sense internal, a self-reflection, is also public. It is a formal address to the audience. The figure and the stage in general offers itself to be read.

The other, related, model is that of the moral biography. Perhaps the most famous example of this is the collection of writings, *A Mirror for Magistrates* (1559). The fictional frame of this book is that its editor, William Baldwin, has gathered together some learned friends. They have searched their way through the history books (the Chronicles) to find figures whose lives and deaths may hold important lessons for the day, for the 1560s. After a short introduction of each figure by Baldwin, who reports on the reasons for choosing them, the various kings, queens and aristocrats as it were walk onto the page and address the reader. They tell their story (in verse) and analyse their lives. They talk about ambition, about God and the devil, and they warn the reader not to make the same mistakes. The Elizabethans (like their predecessors) saw history as an important source of examples of behaviour, for use in their present day.[8]

Contrast Hamlet's 'To be...' soliloquy a matter of minutes earlier in the play's running. He, too, is torn between opposing options. But for one thing, they are not the conventional options of good and evil. And for another, Hamlet has to struggle intellectually to fathom out what the options are. The speech seems to follow a train of thought. We get the sense of a mind working by associations rather than by strictly logical steps. Importantly, the audience has no very secure sense of who or what Hamlet 'is'. We know Claudius fairly well. To put it crudely and in terms appropriate to a later theatrical tradition (of melodrama), he is a villain.[9] But Hamlet is - very famously - much more of an enigma. He even seems not fully to understand himself.

We see, in this speech and others like it, Shakespeare and his contemporaries fashioning a new form of dramatic speech, that of the private individual. By comparison with the Claudius speech, it is as if we as audience look in on Hamlet's private musings.

It is only a little paradoxical that this unknowability is the basis for the feeling by the Romantics and many of us since that Hamlet is much more immediate as a stage figure than is, say, Claudius. It is perhaps simply a question of the sort of immediacy. A figure from the *Mirror*, or an Everyman, had a sort of moral immediacy for their time and culture. We tend not to value such formal, abstracted notions of persons now. They no longer seem authentic - though it is important to remember that they did. We, rather, in our consumption of television, stage plays and films, and the sort of novel that was fashioned last century and remains strong in popular fiction today, tend to find the particular person, with their idiosyncrasies and private motivations, more significant, more true. Indeed, the more private the thoughts appear, the more true they feel.

At this point I want to return to the observation that Shakespeare and others of his generation wrote very ragged plays. The fact is that *Hamlet* contains speeches adhering to quite different conventions, bundled together within the space of a few pages, a few minutes on stage. A way of developing a consideration of this issue is to return to Hamlet's famous soliloquy.

It is essential to attend not simply to what is said in it, or even where it comes in the course of the overall action, but to focus hard first on how it is staged. In order to do this, while for the most part we have to speculate about what playing conventions actually were around 1600 - and Hamlet's advice to the players has been well used in such speculations - we can ask one very sharp and useful question about the soliloquy: what surrounds it, how is it framed?

Consider what editors have designated as the opening of Act 3, the action immediately preceding 'To be..'. Claudius and Gertrude quiz Rosencrantz and Guildenstern about their dealings with Hamlet: how do they read him? With difficulty, they say. The young men then introduce the news of the players being at court. In a way this is a simple piece of plotting on Shakespeare's part: the action is moved forwards, events are made to develop. It is a sort of crossing of neutral territory to get to the showdown.

But it is also much more than this, even this apparently neutral piece of dialogue. It shows the King and Queen trying to manipulate events. The discussion of Hamlet's readability is followed by a brief discussion with Polonius about the plan to have Hamlet secretly observed while meeting Ophelia. The action is available in playing as what the Elizabethans would call a figure - something like a clear and abstractable picture to which one might be able to put a simple title. So as well as a simple piece of lubrication of the plot, we have the figure of royal manipulation.

How else is Claudius figured in *Hamlet*? There is little doubt that the play, like others of its period, assumes that Claudius will appear in some scenes in state. A simple throne, possibly with a canopy, is an efficient way of indicating, on a relatively bare stage as at the Globe, either the majesty of kings, or the trappings of state that persuade people of that majesty. We may presume that Claudius first appears in the play, in Act 1 Scene 2, in state. He formally addresses his court, first as a whole, and then individually.

What that scene does is to show majesty staging itself. Claudius is new to the throne, and he uses his right to address the court to negotiate his way out of possible difficulties. The first thing he does is to try to head off criticisms about the hasty dynastic marriage he and Gertrude have undertaken. His words make an elegant link between the death of old Hamlet and the recent wedding. He speaks with measure; gives first place to grief; and produces the sense that the marriage has happened as the result of mature and caring consideration. He has measured up 'discretion' (wise, logical thinking) against 'nature' (the felt need for sorrow). Thus he not only thereby claims that he has indeed suffered grief over the death, but also links his personal grief with that of the nation. It is almost as if the marriage has been contracted despite a reluctance bred by sorrow.

The question of emotion versus reason is, of course, an important one in relation to the character Hamlet. It is possible to see the theme illustrated through or extended into other characters and bigger structures, like scenes, of the play. But the fact that the whole question of emotional measure becomes a theme of the play in general should not distract us from the rhetorical claims made by Claudius about it here. I mean to suggest that the significant question is not between the opposing claims of reason and emotion but about the politics made out of that opposition, or that relationship. It is tied up with the question of public and private persons.

Claudius goes on in this first court scene to stage a private, feeling, self. After he has attended with calm and efficient authority to the threat from young Fortinbras, he takes time to let the court see him act in a loving and fatherly way towards Laertes. The audience in the theatre are watching two shows. At one level, there is the broad fictional scene of a court in Denmark. Within this, there is the figure of a monarch putting on another show - that of the monarch as loving father to his nation.

It is Hamlet, then, who interrupts Claudius's show. It is possible to read the scene and remark simply that Hamlet is depressed and suspicious, and then to speculate about the rights, wrongs and consequences of this. But let us first attend to what is staged. Claudius attempts to embrace Hamlet with words: 'But now, my cousin, Hamlet, and my son' (1.2.64). The words pretend to be a personal, loving embrace. But what has just happened on stage helps us see that they are an attempt to embrace (include, trap) Hamlet within Claudius's production of himself as a natural and safe figure of authority. Hamlet refuses this. He confounds the language of majesty, and the language of love that majesty appropriates to itself: 'A little more than kin, and less than kind...' (1.2.65). And what follows is another staging, and one that must be attended to at both the levels I have tried here to establish: the staging of characters to one another; and the staging of the fiction in the playhouse. Hamlet's response to Gertrude, 'Seems, madam? Nay, it is. I know not "seems"...' (1.2.76) is a beautifully crafted speech which in a few lines gives clues to an emotional attitude, a disposition. Looked at in one way, it is the beginning of a journey into Hamlet's mind and persona. We can become fascinated by the question of Hamlet. But of primary significance, I want to argue, is the fact that this inside-ness, this interiority, is placed in the scene as something with an authority which challenges that of the state (and together with this, its uses of language and the ways in which it thinks or stages people). The juxtaposition is in itself something like a formal picture, a figure.

The questions are not abstract or general or universal ones about reason and emotion, or personal or character ones about reason and emotion either: they are political and historical questions about the claims of personal power and responsibility, both in leaders and in the led.

Nor are there any genuine interpretative problems about whether Hamlet is really mad or just playing mad. Rather, the play is scripted to present an audience with a problematic: not a crossword for solution, but a web of sometimes contradictory signals that force thought and reflection. The enigma of Hamlet's person is an important player in this. And it should remain. In writing about the play we should not seek to find out the truth of it, but to find out the questions it is asking.

I have raised these general questions out of a consideration of how what happens in the first scenes affects the way in which we view the rest of the play. Those scenes set up not only the story but also a stage language - or rather, a set of stage languages. And the shape of this set of stage languages is, I am suggesting, as much what the play is about as are the fictional events.

To return then to the staging of the 'To be...' soliloquy. At the opening of Act 3 there is a figure of regal manipulation, as there is in Act 1 Scene 2. But this time the figure shows a decay in confidence on the part of Claudius. Hamlet's staging of a private self has robbed Claudius of certainty. He must try to read Hamlet right, to delve into the region Hamlet has declared inaccessible, unknowable.

There is a clash of wills, of imperatives. And both involve the manipulation of appearances; both depend on the ability of shows to move people. Hamlet intends to put on a show, in order to trap Claudius. But Claudius also plans to put on a show, to trap Hamlet. Claudius's show is Ophelia. It is this show which is the setting for the 'To be, or not to be' soliloquy. It is easy to miss this on the page, especially since the speech is so famous as to draw attention to itself, and because editorial notes make so much of its difficulty. The very modern speech is given next to a very conventional, formal piece of staging - a picture of devotion. Shakespeare puts these two dramatic registers in collision with one another. I do not intend to suggest a definite meaning for this collision: but I will claim that it, and other similar collisions, must contribute in a significant way to our understanding of, and feelings about, the play.

In this scene Ophelia is like an object in the hands of the other courtiers. She barely speaks until Hamlet and she meet - except, significantly, the words 'Madam, I wish it may' (3.1.42). She appears honest, sincere and dutiful. Then, her father makes a picture of her on much the same lines. She is given a book to hold, to make her being alone seem motivated. Hamlet must meet her as if she were at her devotion - studying holy words. It as if Ophelia appears twice on stage - once for herself and once as staged by her father. In both instances, she appears modest and sincere. But one of the instances is a fiction, a trap. Noting this need not make us suspect her motives. But the juxtaposition of these two sorts of staging force the question, right at the moment of Hamlet's musings, about how we read the signs given us. Hamlet himself, for instance, has to decide on how to read the Ghost in Act 1. I will return to this later.

But to stay with this scene, let us note that there is an audience on stage. Claudius says that he and Polonius, as fathers to Ophelia and to the nation, may lawfully spy on her and Hamlet. What they see, however, is something that they cannot understand. At the very least, Polonius and Claudius disagree as to whether Hamlet's behaviour has to do with love for Ophelia. Claudius can only think that it has to do with 'something in his soul / Over which his melancholy sits on brood' (3.1.166-7). Claudius is here projecting his guilt, thinking perhaps that Hamlet may have found him out. But he is also caught in a situation in which he still has no secure knowledge about the internal workings of the minds of those whom he as monarch must seek to control.

Hamlet's 'To be...' soliloquy follows shortly on the one at the end of Act 2 (2.2.543-601). In that, he reflects on the power of the players to move people to tears and to action, not only by using fictions, but also by using rather old-fashioned ways of making stories on stage. The object-lesson of being moved leads him to reflect on and upbraid himself for his own inaction; and then to upbraid himself again, this time for simply upbraiding himself and not getting on with things. And from this very nicely written and imagined spiral of ineffectual reflection, Shakespeare has him hit on the ruse of 'The Mousetrap'. The speech ends as a rather conventional planning monologue: 'The play's the thing / Wherein I'll catch the conscience of the King' (2.2.600-1).

The 'To be...' soliloquy develops the reflective elements of this speech, takes Hamlet and his audience in the theatre into speculations about the point of human existence, about personal responsibilities. (I think, by the way, that he is quite clearly raising this question first, and the possibility of suicide only secondarily.) This extension is important, and it is supported precisely by the new sort of psychological writing that we see Shakespeare helping develop here. But equally, Shakespeare plots it so that this rather enigmatic, difficult speech is the one that Claudius overhears. It indeed develops the plot: it makes it necessary that a second overhearing happen, consequently Polonius is killed, and so on. But it is also an important figure for the power that this new stress on the nature of individuals, and what is significant about them, holds around 1600. Shakespeare is not only interested in what we would now call the psychology of his characters. He is also interested in the meaning and value of this new interest in itself. And here he stages this interest, shows us its political importance.

The speech takes place against the foil of a conventionally produced figure of devotion or patience, that of Ophelia. It is a beautiful touch when Hamlet reads that constructed image as transparent, uncomposed. After telling himself, or his thoughts, 'Soft you now' (3.1.88), he turns to her and simply says 'The fair Ophelia' (3.1.89).

It is as if he at the one moment both gives the formal figure its title and reads it as natural. The picture of Ophelia has a value to him, at least. And this is consistent with the difficulty we have, and must remain having, in deciding on his motivations when he tells her to get to a nunnery.[10]

What I am trying to develop the sense of here might be called an economy of difference between two stage languages, two ways of realising people on stage (and, by implication, in the rest of life). There is a meaningful interplay between the readable formal figures and the enigmatic psychological depths. The play with this economy of difference goes still further in this scene.

Polonius is made to reflect on the artificiality of the Ophelia figure he has composed:

> 'Tis too much proved, that with devotion's visage
> And pious action we do sugar o'er
> The devil himself.   (3.1.47-49)

And this immediately precipitates a very conventional guilt-speech from Claudius, which many editions give as an aside - the point being not so much that he speaks unheard by the other characters, but more that he speaks directly to the audience:

O 'tis true.
How smart a lash that speech doth give my conscience...
(3.1.49-50)

There are two stage-worlds present at once: one of the drama that grew out of the late Medieval moralities and the moralising biographies; second, a newer, emergent one of psychological motivation and depth. I think it is underselling Shakespeare a great deal to suggest somehow that he is supposedly struggling free from ways of writing that are becoming redundant. He did, later, leave these older formulae behind. But in this play, he still does something exciting with the difference between the ways of making stage truths - and hence political, social, moral ones, too.

A consideration of these issues raises some familiar topics. There is the question of Hamlet's delay. Take the moment when he approaches Claudius from behind in Act 3 Scene 3. This is the moment mentioned above, when Claudius makes a fairly conventional self-confession speech. Hamlet decides not to kill him there and then in case the act sends Claudius to heaven. We may, if we are interested in Hamlet's psychology, also guess that he is finding excuses. But the scene also gives us a figure of 'Traditional target in revenge tragedy meets revenge hero most interesting for his interior motivations'.[11]

At the least, such a reading of the stage images provided by Shakespeare adds to a sense of the values put on, and questions raised by, the delay. For instance, Hamlet has to decide whether particular ghosts were benign spirits of the dead, or deceitful and manipulative manifestations of the devil. But the Ghost presents Hamlet and his audience in the playhouse with another very important question: what sort of narrative are we in, what sort of world? Revenge tragedies driven by an insistent ghost were old hat by the time *Hamlet* was written. But concrete situations in which personal revenge for a wrong done to family or to person was felt to be both a right and a necessity, were still very real - as they are in parts of Europe, the UK even, today.[12]

Hamlet finds himself in a clash of worlds, a clash of systems of truth and of value. And so, with him, did his first audiences. This makes the advice to the players something more than a demand for a more natural way of playing in the way we might understand that demand now. According to Hamlet, at least, the meaning of holding 'the mirror up to nature' is 'to show virtue her feature, scorn her own image...' (3.2.22-3). The proposition in 1600 is still that truthful shows are shows which do not merely copy, but which place value on things. Deep within even this idea of natural playing is the vital residue of a moralising, abstracting, labelling theatre. We do Shakespeare an injustice to forget it. If we remember it, we will not make the sort of banal 'fourth-wall' reading I opened with.[13]

[1] The Arden edition (Jenkins, 1982) gives a good adjudication of the critical debate about the literal meaning of the speech, and indicates the vast weight of paper consumed conducting it.

[2] A spate of books in the 1980s critically examined the 'meaning' of 'Shakespeare' in British culture, looking at the Royal Shakespeare Company, advertising, education, and so on. The debate resumed with the National Curriculum's concentration on Shakespeare as a necessary component of education in English. See, for instance, Holderness (1988).

[3] Famously, for instance, in 1681 Nahum Tate gave *King Lear* a happy ending.

[4] I depend here on a lecture given by Peter Womack, 'The Shakespeare Question is Compulsory', at Loughborough University, 30 January 1991.

[5] For an extended treatment of these issues, see Belsey (1991). For a very brief account of the changes from feudalism to early capitalism, see Wallis (1991).

[6] I have used the term 'conventional' here to mean something like old-fashioned. I put cautionary inverted commas round the word because it is in some ways a misleading one. If we think about it, all theatrical shows depend on conventions, in the sense that we agree to accept the 'reality' of what the players pretend or narrate. See 'Introduction' to Williams (1968) for a brief and famous discussion of this.

[7] For an accessible edition of the play, see Cawley (1977). We can note that the typical human being is assumed to be male.

8 Baldwin published a second edition of his *A Myrroure for Magistrates. Wherein maybe seen by example of other, howe with grevous plagues vices are punished...* in 1563, adding nine characters to the 1559 original. Several further editions followed. A modern edition was made by Lily B. Campbell in 1938. For occasions when Shakespeare seems to be depending *directly* on the *Mirror*, or on the Chronicles of his own period (by Holinshed, Hall, Foxe and Stow), see Bullough (1957-73).

9 The conventional equivalents, the stock types, for Shakespeare would be the usurping duke and the practiser of *realpolitik* (the Machiavel).

10 Incidentally, 'Soft you now' can itself be seen as having grown from conventional stage speech. When Shakespeare wants Gloucester to appear like the wicked 'Vice' of a morality play at the beginning of *Richard III*, he has him first speak of his murderous plots, openly to the audience, and then say, 'Dive, thoughts, down to my soul...' (1.1.41).

11 Claudius is in the attitude of praying.

12 For a classic (and very pro-*Hamlet*) discussion of the relationship between revenge plays and the organisation of justice in the Elizabethan state, see Bowers (1940). Note how the first court scene is sandwiched between the first and second appearances of the Ghost. We watch Claudius's theatre of state having just witnessed the unsettledness of the dead king. Note, too, that Claudius's concerns come to cluster together love, melancholy, privacy, madness and disorderly speech.

13 By 'fourth wall' I mean of course the illusion intended by the Naturalist stage of the late nineteenth century that the audience were 'looking in on' characters who were totally unaware of the presence of an audience. There was no such assumption in Shakespeare's day. Note that if we use capitals, 'Virtue' and 'Scorn' come to look like characters (so-called 'personified abstractions') from a medieval Morality play.

'Guilty Creatures Sitting at a Play': the audience in *Hamlet*

MICHAEL MANGAN

Hamlet is, in part at least, a play about court politics. Theatre and court politics were always closely entwined in the late sixteenth and early seventeenth centuries. Companies of players were licensed by aristocrats and royalty and could only perform with their implicit permission. New plays were scrutinised closely for potential political content by a board of censors presided over by the Master of the Revels. If Claudius had had an alert Master of the Revels at Elsinore, 'The Murder of Gonzago' would never have been put on. But Claudius had courtiers like Polonius, who seems to have acted as a kind of Danish Master of the Revels, and so 'The Murder of Gonzago', with all its damning attack upon the reigning monarch, slipped through.

In the real world, too, things sometimes slipped through, and plays did occasionally get staged which were politically subversive or personally offensive to nobles or royalty. When this happened, someone was usually punished; more often than not it was the playwright and sometimes the actors too.

Hamlet slipped 'The Murder of Gonzago' past the censor's eye because it was not a new script, but an old one. Hamlet saw the contemporary political relevance of a hoary old play, and staged it, with a few additional speeches, so that it would speak to the immediate situation in Elsinore. This, too, was something that could happen in the actual world of Elizabethan theatre and Elizabethan politics. In February 1601, for example, the Earl of Essex marched on London in an armed rebellion against Elizabeth. One of his co-conspirators, Sir Gelly Meyrick, convinced Shakespeare's theatre company, the Lord Chamberlain's Men, to blow the dust off a hoary old play of their own and stage it as a rallying-cry for Essex's faction. Persuaded by the £2 bribe he offered them, they agreed to put on, at very short notice, a special performance of a play which showed a corrupt old monarch being deposed by a vigorous young rebel: Shakespeare's *Richard II*, written about six years earlier. When Essex's rebellion failed miserably, the only surprise was that neither Shakespeare nor the Lord Chamberlain's Men were themselves punished. They got off lightly: Essex and many of his co-conspirators (including Shakespeare's own patron, the Earl of Southampton) were condemned to death.

At least one of Shakespeare's colleagues in the Lord Chamberlain's Men had been against the idea in the first place - or so he said afterwards. Augustine Phillips had complained that *Richard II* was 'so old and so long out of use that they should have small or no company at it'. Presumably the £2 bribe overcame his objection, but Phillips was speaking as a man of the theatre. In order to complete the meaning of a play it is necessary to have an audience. Each audience brings to a performance a series of assumptions and preconceptions, its own concerns and its own ways of making meanings. A skilful playwright understands this, and understands too that a play's meaning is created in the interaction between what an audience already knows (or thinks it knows) and what it is offered by the play it sees. Nor is any single audience completely homogeneous: it is possible to aim different parts of play at different parts of an audience, or different levels of meaning at different levels of understanding. In this way, Hamlet's staging of 'The Murder of Gonzago' is different from Sir Gelly Meyrick's *Richard II*. The Essex conspirators envisaged the play acting as a catalyst for a whole audience to realise, together, the analogy between Richard and Elizabeth. It is the fantasy shared by the most naive kind of political playwright and the censor - that the performance will spark the revolution. But Hamlet has another aim: he is interested not in the audience *en masse* but in one particular member of the audience. If his suspicions are correct, 'The Murder of Gonzago' will 'catch the conscience of the King' (2.2.601) because Claudius has a special kind of knowledge which he will bring to the performance, and he will read that performance in a particular way; it will have meanings for him that it cannot have for any 'innocent' member of the audience.

In this essay I will be looking at ways in which the different audiences for whom Shakespeare was writing may have conditioned what he wrote. I suspect that one of the reasons that Shakespeare

seems to be 'not for an age but for all time' is that he learned
comparatively early in his development as a dramatist the skill of
constructing a play so that it would offer different things to different
audiences. In the case of *Hamlet* this means primarily the audience at
the Globe theatre in London, and to audience in the provinces.

When *Hamlet* first appeared in print in a poor Quarto version in
1603, it bore the following title-page:

> THE / Tragicall Historie of HAMLET / Prince of Denmarke /
> By William Shake-speare. / As it hath beene diuerse times acted
> by his Highnesse ser- / uants in the Cittie of London: as also in
> the two V- / niuersities of Cambridge and Oxford, and elsewhere
> / At London printed for N.L. and Iohn Trundell.

By 1603, it seems, *Hamlet* had been acted by the Lord
Chamberlain's Men (who were re-named 'His Highnesse seruants'
when King James came to the throne that year) in London, Cambridge
and Oxford, 'and elsewhere'. The London performance would have
been at the Globe. The others would have been staged as part of the
regular tours which all the main London companies undertook during
the summer, when the London theatres closed down.

That *Hamlet* should have been played at the Universities of Oxford
and Cambridge seems particularly fitting. Tragedies had always been
at home in the universities, of course. College Halls had long been
used for the staging of plays, both by undergraduate actors and by
travelling professional companies. University drama itself was an
important element in the growth of the Elizabethan theatre: it was
through the universities that classical influences such as that of
Seneca found their way onto the popular stage - and *Hamlet* was a
play much influenced by Senecan drama. Many of the playwrights of
the Elizabethan and Jacobean eras were themselves university-
educated (though not Shakespeare), and the Elizabethan stage had
even produced a major tragedy whose protagonist was an academic:
Marlowe's Doctor Faustus was a fellow of Hamlet's own University
of Wittenburg. *Hamlet*, however, is the only major tragedy of the
period to have an undergraduate as a hero.

In some ways Hamlet is a caricature of the young scholar. His
language is erudite, his range of reference wide; his quick-witted
replies, his continual play of intellect all attest his status as a man of
education. Early on in the play Claudius's remark about Hamlet's

desire to return 'to school in Wittenberg' (1.2.113) establishes Hamlet's position and status. When he first learns of Claudius's crime, he calls for his 'tables' (1.5.107) in order to set down his discovery that 'one may smile, and smile, and be a villain' (108). At times he plays the role of absent-minded scholar quite deliberately, incorporating it into his mask of madness as he wanders the corridors of Elsinore immersed in a book, reading 'Words, words, words' (2.2.192).

There is, it is true, one detail which throws Hamlet's undergraduate status into a more ambiguous light: the indeterminacy about his age. The computations of Hamlet's age within the play put him, according to the gravedigger, as a thirty-year old undergraduate: a mature student by today's standards and even more so by the norms of Shakespeare's day, when a more usual age for a young man to go up to University would have been sixteen. Yet, paradoxically, his youth is emphasised several times in the play: 'young Hamlet' (1.1.175) he is called by his friend Horatio; Polonius agrees that 'he is young' (1.4.124); Claudius and Gertrude, of course, treat 'this mad young man' (4.1.19) as if he were a boy - but so does his apparent contemporary Laertes, who talks of Hamlet's love for Ophelia as 'A violet in the youth of primy nature' (1.3.7).

The matter hardly seems to be a crucial one, although it has bothered many readers, and perhaps was at the root of some of those critical approaches to the play which show such immense distaste for this 'immature' thirty-year old who behaves like an adolescent. And it is difficult to ignore the overall impression that *Hamlet* is a tragedy which has to do with youth, just as *King Lear* is one which has to do with old age. More precisely, perhaps, Hamlet focuses on a young man in a society which is ruled by old men; *King Lear* concentrates on an old man in a society which is being taken over by the next generation.

There are two main possibilities concerning the contradictory information we are given about Hamlet's age: one is quite simply that Shakespeare was being a little careless, and did not realise that he was effectively contradicting himself. This is perfectly possible - there are many instances of similar carelessness in the plays - but it is not entirely likely in this instance. Shakespeare seems very insistent on the thirty-year period, and the Gravedigger establishes it by two separate calculations: the first involves his own period of service as gravedigger, which dates from the day of Hamlet's birth and comes to thirty years; the second concerns the skull of Yorick, which 'hath lien you i'th' earth three and twenty years' (5.1.165-6) - Yorick the jester with whom Hamlet played as a boy. The notion of a thirty-year-old Hamlet seems firmly established here. And so it is worth considering the other possibility - that the play's contradictions concerning Hamlet's age might have some significance.

We are led to see Hamlet as young in the early stages of the play. It is there that so much emphasis is put upon his youth, as if the writer were trying to establish it as an essential fact about his protagonist. We do not get the contradictory detail about Hamlet being thirty years old until towards the end of the play. Now it may well be that Shakespeare is playing around with time-scales (as he does elsewhere in his plays) in order to make some sort of point - to suggest perhaps that although only a few weeks seem to have gone by in stage time, somehow Hamlet has grown up during that time. This, again, is a possibility, although not one that I like very much. Another interpretative manoeuvre might be to see the contradictions about Hamlet's age as being typical of his character in general: this reading would argue that the difficulty that audiences and other characters in the play have in interpreting his character, are mirrored in this detail, that nobody can even say whether he is young or middle-aged.

There is another way of dealing with the contradiction, however - one which does not resolve it but which leaves it intact. In 1601, when *Hamlet* was most probably written and first performed, Richard Burbage, for whom the part of Hamlet was written, was thirty-four years old. The Hamlet whom the original Elizabethan audiences would have seen on the stage, would not have been an adolescent by any means. This may well explain why the audience is told so frequently, early in the play, that Hamlet is young: a playwright sometimes needs to compensate for the visual effect of his actors. By the end of the play, in a comic scene, Shakespeare is confident enough to be able to acknowledge this fact and admit to his audience that this adolescent prince that they have been watching is actually a grown man of thirty-four - or at any rate, allowing for a small sop to Burbage's vanity, thirty.

At first glance this may seem like a disappointingly prosaic way of explaining the paradox of Hamlet's age, but its importance lies in its acceptance of the constraints of the theatre upon the meaning of the text. It is a truism to say that plays differ from other forms of literature because they are written to be performed rather than read. However, the logic of this entails that the original conditions of performance then dictate (to a certain extent) how the writer fashions the story. In *Hamlet* this is a particularly important element, since in this play more than any other Shakespeare makes the whole business of play-writing and performance central to his plot. The paradox of Hamlet's age hinges on the crucial relationship between events within the fiction itself (the age of the fictional Prince) and events in the 'real world' - the age of the actual actor playing the Prince. Time and time again in *Hamlet*, the audience is confronted with the problem of making sense of the relationship between events in a fictional world and events in a 'real' world, for one of the main themes of the play is theatricality itself.

The Elizabethan theatre was a notoriously self-conscious institution, which enjoyed referring to, and often making jokes about, its own theatricality. But few writers ever dealt with this notion as subtly and as comprehensively as Shakespeare did in *Hamlet*. In order to get a sense of the thoroughness of Shakespeare's playing with theatrical illusion and dramatic convention in *Hamlet*, let us look in detail at one extraordinary exchange, which takes place just before that play within a play, and imagine how it must have come across to a contemporary audience in the Globe theatre near the beginning of the seventeenth century. The play is about halfway through. Hamlet is hot on the trail of Claudius, and is about to confirm his suspicions by means of the performance of 'The Murder of Gonzago'. The players are ready, the court is assembling and the tension is mounting. As members of the court take their places in the onstage audience, Hamlet and Polonius have the following exchange:

> *Ham.* My lord, you played once i'th' university, you say?
> *Pol.* That did I, my lord, and was accounted a good actor.
> *Ham.* What did you enact?
> *Pol.* I did enact Julius Caesar. I was killed i'th' Capitol. Brutus
> killed me.
> *Ham.* It was a brute part of him to kill so capital a calf there. Be
> the players ready? (3. 2. 97-105)

What is the point of this short and apparently inconsequential conversation? Why does Shakespeare bother to include it at this moment in the play? These questions can be answered on a number of different levels. First, on the level of theatrical technique: as noted above, the exchange comes at a point when the entire court is assembling on stage in order to watch the Players' performance. As a matter of sheer craftsmanship, Shakespeare would have found it useful to include one or more short and self-contained conversations between characters in order to cover the inevitable hiatus on stage while everybody found their places and sat down.

Second, there is the way in which the exchange contributes to the immediate dramatic action. It comes just after a rather aggressive little clash between Hamlet and Claudius, and for Hamlet to be able to turn away from the King and engage Polonius in trivial small-talk about Polonius's university career allows him, effectively, to snub Claudius.

But what of the actual words spoken? At a third level, they contribute to the character-drawing which goes on in the play. We already know that Polonius is supposed to be a bit of a buffoon - a 'tedious old fool', as Hamlet calls him earlier. Hamlet himself, on the other hand, is a rather sharp-witted young man. This exchange confirms both these characters. People reminiscing about their student days always sound a little fatuous, and Polonius is no exception. The slightly odd way in which he talks about his performance ('*I* was killed i'th' Capitol. Brutus killed *me*'), as if, significantly, he is unable to distinguish between actor and role, adds to our overall impression of his foolishness. Hamlet, conversely, maintains his character of wit and ironist, seizing on Polonius's words and playing with them, using them as counters in a verbal game which allows him to score off Polonius, and eventually to insult him (for 'calf' is a way of saying 'fool').

At yet another level, we might consider the specific implications of these references to Brutus and Caesar. Critics have often pointed to a resemblance between the characters of Hamlet and of Brutus in Shakespeare's *Julius Caesar*: both of them are basically honest men who get caught up in circumstances beyond their control which lead them to commit murders; both of them spend time examining their consciences about the rights and wrongs of their chosen course. So, is Shakespeare effectively asking at this point that the audience make the comparison between Hamlet and Brutus? Almost certainly - and in a very specific way. For there is a further level of irony. Twentieth-century scholars have attempted to compile cast-lists of Shakespeare's plays, and to work out which actors in his original company played which roles. This research is incomplete and there are gaps in the findings, and yet certain agreements have been reached. From these agreements we can build the following picture: the actor playing the role of Hamlet is, as noted above, the thirty-four-year-old Richard Burbage. Opposite him as Polonius is John Heminges (who was later to co-edit the First Folio of Shakespeare's plays.) The same research indicates that when the Chamberlain's Men first staged *Julius Caesar* a year or two earlier (and perhaps when they revived it a week or two earlier) Burbage had played Brutus, and Heminges had played Caesar. So, now, during the performance of *Hamlet*, Heminges/Polonius reminds Burbage/Hamlet that they had previously played opposite each other in the roles of Brutus and Caesar. And thus for a second or two, the actors step out of role, and the audience are forced for that instant, to see them not as Polonius and Hamlet, but as Heminges and Burbage, making a joke about themselves as actors and about the parts they play. And, although we need not discount all the other levels of meaning which I have suggested, what gives the moment its energy is the fact that it operates quite simply as a joke between the two actors.

The Burbage/Heminges joke is more than a theatrical in-joke, of course. First of all, it amplifies one of the central themes of the play. *Hamlet* tells a story about people whose lives are based on kinds of play-acting - Hamlet himself being a character who is obsessed with theatres and play-acting. But at another level, what Shakespeare is doing at this point is destabilising the whole structure of the dramatic fiction. He is saying to the audience 'Don't get too involved - this is a play, remember'. And he is using a whole battery of dramatic techniques in order to do it. On the one hand, we remember, this comes at a moment when the audience is about to see a play within a play, and to watch an audience on stage watching that play. This technique of showing a play within a play is one of the favourite devices of Shakespeare's generation of dramatists (Shakespeare himself had already used it several times before he wrote *Hamlet*) and one of its inevitable results is to bring under scrutiny the whole business of plays and their effects on audiences. Then, as if to compound this, Shakespeare has characters in this very same scene who make reference to *Julius Caesar*, a play which he himself wrote and which the Lord Chamberlain's Men had staged comparatively recently. To add to the irony, Polonius is himself the Lord Chamberlain in Claudius's court. Even at this level the dramatic illusion is by now under some stress. And then, relentlessly, Shakespeare throws in the further level of complexity which involves two actors making a joke about the parts they play. So, at exactly the point in the play when Claudius is about to get so involved in the action of a performance that he loses control and gives himself away, Shakespeare goes to immense lengths to jolt the audience out of their immersion in the dramatic fiction, and to remind them that they are 'creatures sitting at a play.' It is not until later that the audience discover that there is yet another level of irony: just as Burbage/Brutus killed Heminges/Caesar in the earlier play, so Burbage/Hamlet will kill Heminges/Polonius in this one. The brief conversation between Hamlet and Polonius also functions as a moment of dramatic foreshadowing, preparing the way for events to come.

If we take seriously the idea that Shakespeare's plays were written to be acted on the stage rather than to be read in the study, we need to be able to take into account such apparently trivial details as the age of a particular actor, or the fact that an actor may be recognised from one part to another - those details, in short, which have most to do with the presence of an audience. One of the striking features of the drama of the Elizabethan period is the way in which playwrights do address themselves directly to an audience; an awareness of that audience is an integral part of the playwright's art. It is, therefore, not in the least implausible to think of Shakespeare playing directly to an audience in such a way, allowing his actors to make jokes about themselves.

This takes us back, though, to the idea that there is more than one audience for any play. In the case of *Hamlet* we have already identified at least two audiences from the title-page of the first Quarto: there is the audience in 'the Cittie of London' and the audience 'in the two Vniuersities of Cambridge and Oxford'. And different audiences will experience the same play in different ways. The Burbage/Heminges joke is available to the regular patrons of the Globe in a way that it may not have been to the Fellows and undergraduates who watched the play in Oxford and Cambridge. Conversely, perhaps the intellectualism of young Hamlet struck more forcible chords in the college Hall than it did in Globe performances. The drama is a very unstable form of art and a play can undergo shifts in meaning from one performance to the next. It may well be that what the Globe audience 'saw' was a play in which Hamlet came across as a rather brittle and unsympathetic figure, whereas the college audience saw in him a character whose cast of mind it found recognisable and attractive. The various arguments which twentieth-century critics have had about Hamlet's character (whether he is immature and self-indulgent, or whether he is sensitive and sympathetic) might turn out to have been contradictions which were inherent in the play from its earliest performances.

I have argued so far that the metatheatricality of *Hamlet* is very thoroughgoing. As many other critics have done, I have argued that the play is particularly self-aware, and that one of its subjects is its own theatricality. I have tried to add a further dimension to this by showing how the play tends to capitalise on an awareness of the audience, and indeed of different potential audiences. It remains to ask if there is any discernible reason why Shakespeare examines, parodies, explores and dissects the nature of theatricality so intensively in *Hamlet*? It may be, of course, that this merely represents a natural expression of his own interest in the theatre, but it may also be the case that there is some further and more specific cause. This takes us back to the story which began this essay. The exact date of *Hamlet* is uncertain, and so what follows can only be expressed tentatively. Nonetheless, it is probable that the play was substantially written and first performed during 1601 - the same year as the Lord Chamberlain's Men mounted their ill-judged performance of *Richard II*, staged for the benefit of the supporters of the Earl of Essex's abortive rebellion.

That performance of *Richard II* was designed (by Sir Gelly Meyrick at least) to have an effect on the real world of power politics, and to make some difference to the cause of the Earl of Essex. Elizabeth herself recognised the intended identification between herself and Richard, and saw what kind of mirror was being held up to Nature there. Her subsequent leniency towards the Lord Chamberlain's Men must have been experienced by them all with massive relief. There is something particularly daring about writing and performing *Hamlet* immediately after that, given the similarities between the events in fictional Elsinore and those in real-life London. *Hamlet* is, after all, another play which sets a corrupt old ruler against a rebellious young hero. But now, in *Hamlet*, the hero rewrites an old play and puts it on in order to bring about the downfall of the old ruler. And *Hamlet* itself is an old revenge play rewritten by Shakespeare to bring it up to date. If 1601 is a correct date for *Hamlet* it says something about Shakespeare's nerve, if nothing else.

The company of Players who arrive at Elsinore are down-at-heel, their low fortunes ascribed to 'the late innovation' (2.2.331): this 'innovation' is usually taken to be a reference to the ensuing theatrical in-joke about the boy actors who carry the custom of the town. However, as Harold Jenkins explains in his Arden edition of the play, the word 'innovation' could be synonymous with 'rebellion'. To accept this reading of the word immediately presents us with a picture of a company of actors who have fallen on hard times because of a recent rebellion. It is quite possible to see in this a wry reference to what might have happened to Shakespeare's own company in 1601 if Elizabeth had decided to be less lenient. The very fleetingness of the remark lends plausibility to the reading: if it is an allusion to the Chamberlain's Men's brush with power politics, then it is an enigmatic reference, perhaps for the benefit of only a very few hearers, which it may be best not to spell out too clearly.

The aftermath of Essex's fiasco would be precisely the time when Shakespeare would need to do some serious thinking, or re-thinking, about the nature of theatre, and in particular about its relationship with the real world. At the most basic level, the relationship between dramatic illusion and reality which the play probes may be informed by the insistent reality of Shakespeare's own recent career as dramatist. It seems more than probable that the intensive exploration of the nature of theatre which Shakespeare undertakes in *Hamlet* was prompted by the narrow escape which his own company of players had just had. In *Hamlet* what we may well be seeing is a writer attempting to define again for himself the nature, scope and implications of his own art - and taking the risk of doing so in front of that unstable and unpredictable thing, an audience.

On (Re)cycling *Hamlet*:
a consideration of the play's staging

CHRISTINE WHITE

In 1899, Kawakami, a Japanese amateur actor and raconteur, visited Europe and the United States. Although he had no training in the techniques of kabuki, a type of traditional Japanese theatre, he appeared in kabuki plays in San Francisco, New York, and Paris, much to the dismay of Japanese residents who were familiar with kabuki plays. Kawakami saw himself as a theatrical missionary bringing kabuki to the west and, conversely, western drama to Japan as, on his return, he staged a production of a play from the European tradition. Predictably the play was *Hamlet*; equally predictably, he took the title role.

Legend has it that in one scene he made his entrance on a bicycle. In the same way that American and European audiences who had attended performances were deceived into thinking that what they were seeing was kabuki, so Japanese audiences were misled into thinking that Kawakami's production of *Hamlet* represented western theatre. Hamlet on a bicycle was not incongruous to a Japanese audience of that period, for both *Hamlet* and the bicycle were new and foreign and therefore logically belonged together. *Hamlet* is not foreign to us, but the intervening hundred years have seen a good many more incongruous performances than a cycling Hamlet.

There is no definitive way of presenting *Hamlet*. This is a cause for celebration. In Shakespeare's writing, as in that of most dramatists, there is always space for interpretation; but perhaps in the case of Shakespeare more than other dramatists one can always find something new and thus a new staging can always be found dependent on what is considered to be important and relevant. A particular staging is a method of conveying a particular interpretation of the play. It doesn't take the play over; rather, it highlights a particular interest in what the play has to offer.

Film versions of *Hamlet* made by Laurence Olivier in 1948 and Franco Zeffirelli in 1991, while using the same medium, depict and locate scenes differently. Each presents a different feel for *Hamlet* and the atmosphere of the location of Elsinore. These differences are even more apparent in theatrical interpretations of the play. In this medium there are endless styles of performance and many and varied stage spaces in which *Hamlet* could be staged - from the spectacular Minack theatre in the rocks on the coast of Cornwall, to a pub theatre such as the Bush in London. The specific space in which a piece is going to be performed has a crucial effect on the interpretation.

The design and features of the Globe Theatre, the space in which many of Shakespeare's plays were performed, were carefully chosen. The first Globe Theatre of 1599 was designed by actors based on their understanding of what worked for the kinds of plays they performed. The choices they made in terms of architectural features determined their performance style and the pace of the production. It also informed the type of presentation which was most suitable for this theatre building. Therefore the scenographic elements bore a direct relation to the space. It is also important to recognise that the Globe worked as a commercial space producing new plays regularly. It is likely that the plays would therefore be required almost to direct themselves around the space.

The first Elizabethan public playhouse in London opened in 1576 and was most aptly and simply named - the Theatre. When James Burbage undertook to build the Theatre he had two sources of information on which to draw for the design of the theatre building and its stage areas: first, the known features which had been effective for theatrical presentation for hundreds of years; second, the structural elements in public and private buildings in which actors had performed up until this time. Burbage combined both sources and the design served as a model for public playhouses built in London during the period up to the English Civil War in 1642. The similarity between the design of the Theatre and that of the Globe would have been considerable. For, when the Theatre was pulled down in 1599 its timbers and other building materials were used in the construction of the Globe. Remarkably, the design has been influential in theatre architecture in the latter part of this century.

A further influence undoubtedly came from John Braynes who was Burbage's father-in-law and one of the financial backers in the building of the Theatre. Nine years previously, John Braynes engaged a carpenter, William Sylvester, to make 'theatrical provisions' at The Red Lion in Stepney (Orrell, 1988: 20). The original Red Lion building was not, as one might assume, an inn but possibly a farm. Documents suggest that there was a new and independent structure including a stage with a void space in the stage floor for a trap door, a turret, and surrounding galleries . All the features of this space are consistent with what came later in the theatre for which Shakespeare was to write, the Globe. John Braynes thus established the pattern of the Elizabethan theatre long before the earliest records of the use of innyards for the staging of plays in London. He brought his experience of building The Red Lion to the construction of the Theatre.

Up until 1599 Shakespeare was writing plays for the type of stages found in the innyards, the Theatre and possibly the Curtain, London's second purpose-built playhouse which opened in 1577. Once the Globe had been built, Shakespeare could take advantage of more efficient and effective means of production and the opportunities for elaborate staging.

The Elizabethan public playhouses were first and foremost a space in which to erect a stage and enclose an audience. Burbage was without doubt influenced by the amphitheatrical plan taken from Greek and Roman classical theatre. This model was already present in the structure of the bear-baiting rings on the south side of the Thames. Burbage adapted the example of the bear-garden in having three levels on which to sit. Within the galleries were tiers of benches, with standing room at the highest level at the back; partitions of varying heights divided the tiers into sections. These sections have evolved into the boxes situated near the stage, for example at the Metropolitan Opera House, New York, the Royal Opera House, Covent Garden, and the Theatre Royal, Nottingham. The yard area surrounding the platform stage on three sides was most probably raked (sloped), so as to allow for water drainage and provide better visibility for those seated in the first level of the gallery.

The stage contained traps for special effects. The texts of Shakespeare's plays of this period suggest there may have been up to five traps. A small one at each of the four corners, capable of carrying one person, and one long narrow one across the centre which could perhaps bear as many as eight people and/or elaborate and heavy properties. The traps were very noisy to operate and to cover the noise, there is often a stage direction for music, thunder, blasts on wind instruments, or a drum roll (see fig. 1). The music would have been played from the musicians' gallery. This was the third tier above the stage and had poor visibility from the auditorium so would not have been needed much as an acting area. The sound effects of thunder and of battles would have been operated in the huts (see fig. 2). In the huts the rolling of a cannon ball down an incline would reverberate like thunder, and fireworks and a small cannon would be fired for the enactment of a battle. Also inside the huts were mechanisms for flying illusions; it is conceivable that actors would be flown for certain roles: possibly the fairies in *A Midsummer Night's Dream* and Ariel in *The Tempest* (see fig. 3).

The stage was backed and roofed. This allowed for entrance and exit doors and protection from inclement weather. The carved screen of the great hall of a wealthy patron, with its two doors at the side, formed the source of this feature. The stage facade resembled a three-storied Elizabethan house topped by a gabled attic rising above the roof and the third gallery. In the centre of this facade at stage level was a curtained alcove which formed an inner stage. This had a door to the audience's right and a window in the back wall to the audience's left. The door could open and reveal the foot of the staircase leading to the second storey, which also had a curtained alcove in the centre. These alcoves resemble the modern box set, but instead of solid walls the Elizabethan set had curtains.

There is considerable academic debate about the nature of the inner stage and the uses to which it might have been put. There are no definitive conclusions to the debate, but one might imagine that there were three ways in which the alcove at stage level could have been used: first, as an interior in its own right; second, as an extension of an interior scene signified by placing set or objects further down stage such as a throne or a bed; third, as a backing to a scene played further down stage with the curtains closed or used as an arras. This may have been used in *Hamlet* to conceal Polonius in the Queen's bedchamber. In the floor of the inner stage, as this alcove is sometimes called, was a long narrow trap door known as the grave. This could be used for ghostly apparitions or for descents to a vault or underground prison. In *Hamlet* it might have been used for the 'gravediggers' scene and the burial of Ophelia. The second-storey curtained gallery would also have been used as an acting area. In *Hamlet* it is conceivable that scenes on the battlements might have been played there.

The timbers used in the building determined that the shape of the theatre was octagonal. Its octagonal shape offered two other areas for acting and these were window bays. They could be used to represent houses. Supported by slender columns, they looked separate from the stage area and resembled in architectural form Tudor domestic dwellings. This would have been the acting area used for the staging of the balcony scene from *Romeo and Juliet*. Balconies of this nature in more modern theatre buildings are always referred to as Juliets.

All these features offered different levels, platforms, spaces and balconies on which to perform the scenes. The variety of settings afforded quick changes in location from scene to scene with little formal scenery changing as we understand it. As a performance space it was flexible and variable allowing for continuous staging. The flexibility of the multi-stage setting of the Elizabethan theatre is something which theatre designers in the twentieth century often have striven to recreate (see fig. 4).

A knowledge of the features of the Elizabethan stage is essential to an understanding of the original performance context. The modern production team has different choices to make about the presentation of Shakespeare's plays. Radical changes have occurred in theatre architecture in the past hundred years alone. What is considered valuable in a theatre building varies for many reasons; it may vary because of the changing fashions of the time and differing concepts of theatre-going as a social activity, or because of the development of a performance theory, or because of imported influences from other cultures. Thus the formality of the proscenium arch theatres built from the latter half of the nineteenth century (such as the Theatre Royal, Nottingham) or the more open and flexible arrangements of some more recent twentieth-century theatres (such as the Leicester Haymarket or Nottingham Playhouse) are historically determined and serve(d) contemporary needs, concepts, and styles of staging presentation.

Before there can be a consideration of the possibilities of a modern design for *Hamlet*, it is necessary to go back to the play and decide what is appropriate and necessary for an interpretation of the play. One way of determining this is to note the location and significant action of each scene:

Act 1
  sc 1   The guard platform of the castle
  sc 2   The castle
  sc 3   Polonius's house
  sc 4   The guard platform of the castle
  sc 5   The battlements of the castle (Ghost reportedly beneath stage)

Act 2
  sc 1   Polonius's house
  sc 2   The castle

Act 3
  sc 1   The castle
  sc 2   The castle (play within the play)
  sc 3   The castle
  sc 4   The queen's closet (Polonius behind the arras. Hamlet draws arras, before exit has to get Polonius's body off stage)

Act 4
  sc 1   The castle
  sc 2   The castle
  sc 3   The castle
  sc 4   A plain in Denmark (Fortinbras and army cross stage)
  sc 5   The castle (Laertes's noisy entry, the doors are broken)
  sc 6   The castle
  sc 7   The castle

Act 5
  sc 1   A churchyard (Gravedigger digs and throws up skulls from grave; Hamlet leaps into grave and fights Laertes.)
  sc 2   The castle (shots and sound of advancing army ; play ends with peals of ordinance shot off.)

What is apparent is that the predominant location is the castle, but often no specific area of the castle is indicated. Consequently, a director or designer might then make a choice that the scenes in the castle are taking place in all manner of nooks and crannies and not the interior of the castle as a single space that appears repeatedly. The rapid scene changes following Polonius's killing might militate in favour of this concept. Though there are relatively few locations, what is needed is an almost continual sense of movement around the interior of different parts of the castle. This in itself is an interpretation of the need of the play and consequently would inform the way in which I personally would approach designing the set. This is, however, only one way of approaching the design; there are, of course, many others.

Although it is hard to categorise design, it may be helpful to consider ways we can describe the setting of a play, remembering that many pieces of visual art extend into more than one area of classification. The following ways of distinguishing design constitute different interpretations and will derive from individual producers, directors and designers' approaches to the play. The choices made will determine the style or method of production. It is also important to bear in mind that in addition to personal choice, the categories are also influenced by the specific theatre space in which the production will take place. What is offered below represents five useful categories when thinking about design:

1) as utilitarian - that is we are presented with a setting that offers the workable approach to the play, what we need in order to function through the play

2) as a presentation - to directly convey the actual world of the play, an actual castle, a grave yard and the house of Polonius.

3) as a machine - the set becomes a workable moving unit, which the actors operate to 'produce' the play.

4) as an environment - a space is created to play out the drama, which is conducive to the action and desired themes or concepts.

5) as a statement - the design embodies a meaning or 'the' meaning of the play.

All of these are possible interpretations which could be applied to *Hamlet*.

In terms of the above categories, Elizabethan staging might be thought of as a utilitarian set in which the actual theatre is the setting. It is ideal for creating a fast moving piece of theatre where the characters wander the corridors of Elsinore. There are doors which characters can pass through whilst plotting their next move. There are different levels from which characters, for instance, can look out across the battlements, and enclosed spaces for the more intimate scenes. The open stage provides a battlefield and, with the use of the grave trap, the churchyard. The performance is continuous, uninterrupted by scene changes.

Since the Elizabethan period, western theatre has gone through many different styles and this evolution has brought about a variety of different buildings and staging arrangements. The Lyceum theatre of 1864 had a vastly different concept of design from the Elizabethan public playhouse like the Globe. Charles Fechter played Hamlet in front of a series of painted backdrops, the majority of which were designed and executed by the distinguished scenic artist, William Telbin. Location was thus created by these realistic painted backcloths. Between each act the curtain would drop in order to allow the painted scene to be changed. This practice was the antithesis of the fluid and continuous staging possible on the Elizabethan stage. Entertainment during these scene changes was provided by a band which would strike up between each act. It played a variety of music to accompany this production of *Hamlet*: *Don Juan* by Mozart formed the opening overture; the *William Tell Overture* by Rossini ended Act 3; and 'Vivi Tu' from Donizetti's *Anna Bolena* ended the play. The scenery was beautifully painted and an audience would have visited the play to see the sets as much as to watch *Hamlet*. This was spectacle theatre and actor-managers like Fechter relied on spectacular theatrical effect to get their audience in. For instance, he used the Pepper's Ghost effect for the ghostly apparition. This involves the actor being beneath the stage, probably in the orchestra pit; he is lit in such a way that the reflection of the actor appears as a transparent image on a piece of glass situated between the audience and the stage.

In 1892 Herbert Beerbohm Tree staged *Hamlet*. During this period several managers deemed it essential that all theatrical settings should be both historically and archaeologically correct. The recent invention and use of electric light in theatres highlighted the paintings, as opposed to the general murk of gaslight in which they had previously been presented. Telbin's painting for this production, whilst of course a two-dimensional image, took some inspiration from features of the Elizabethan stage. It offered a representation, for instance, of a raised room at the back of the stage before which the players could perform before the assembled court. Obviously it was felt necessary to present this in a special space. The effect of a play within a play was quite literally echoed in the stage presentation, as it is in the text of *Hamlet* itself. The upstage area was painted to suggest the Elizabethan inner alcove or inner stage, thus offering a room behind the action. The costumes for the production were a Victorian interpretation of the period in which *Hamlet, Prince of Denmark* is set, around 1200 A.D.

In 1911, a seminal early twentieth-century designer and theorist, Edward Gordon Craig was asked to design a production of *Hamlet* for the Moscow Arts Theatre. Craig took a very different point of view from that represented by the theatre of Fechter and Beerbohm Tree. Craig's theory hinged on his principle that, 'When producing great drama, I have never been concerned in any attempt to show the spectators an exact view of some historical period in architecture. I always feel that all great plays have an order of architecture which is more or less theatrical, unreal as the play' (quoted in Bablet, 1981: 188). Craig had been an actor with Henry Irving's company at the Lyceum and had seen the shortcomings of gas-lit, two-dimensional settings. He was influenced by Herbert von Herkomer, a scenic artist who questioned many features of contemporary theatre. Herkomer noted that the angle of viewing from the upper balconies of most theatres made the actors appear foreshortened, the footlights cast unnatural shadows on the actors' faces, the quality of the painted scenery was flat and lifeless. He demonstrated that atmospheric effects could be achieved by using electric lights, lantern slides and gauzes.

Craig and Constantin Stanislavsky, the Russian director of the 1911 *Hamlet*, had conceived the play as a 'monodrama' in which Hamlet was the only real person, all others were only imagined by him. The audience were thus to see events through Hamlet's eyes. The design included a system of screens that moved into various positions about the stage. For the time this was extremely innovative. The screens were architectonic forms which moved in all directions at any tempo and theoretically could create endlessly variable scenic environments which could be coloured with electric light or decorated with projections. However, Craig was not an engineer and the screens did not move easily. Consequently they were ill suited to

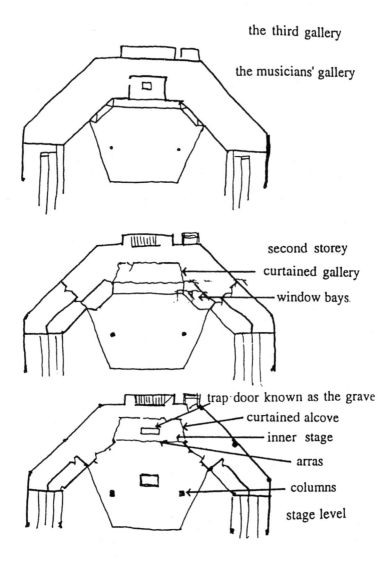

Figure 1. Diagram of features of an Elizabethan public playhouse. (*Drawing by Christine White*)

Fig.2

Fig.3

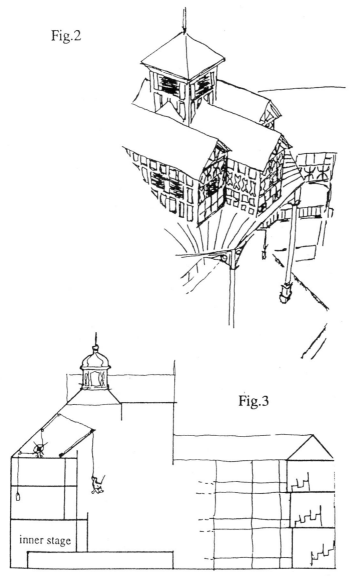

inner stage

Figures 2 & 3. The second Globe Theatre - Fig. 2 from above, showing the huts rising above the gabled attic; Fig. 3 in section, showing the mechanism used for flying
(*Drawings by Christine White*)

Figure 4. The Second Globe Theatre
(*Drawing by Christine White*)

Figures 5 & 6. The Players Scene, *Hamlet.* The Royal
Shakespeare Company - Fig.5 *(top)* The Other Place, Stratford
on Avon, directed by Buzz Goodbody, 1975; Fig.6 *(bottom)* The
Barbican, London, directed by Adrian Noble, 1992.
*(Figures 5&6 Copyright - Shakespeare Centre Library:
Joe Cocks Studio Collection)*

Figure 7. The construction site of the third Globe Theatre, Southbank, London, 1993. (*Photograph by Christine White*)

the scenic fluidity which *Hamlet* demands.

Craig did not want a curtain to hide scene changes but used visible scene setters who would make the audience conscious they were watching a symbolic rather than a realistic performance. However, the screens were so precarious that the curtains had to be drawn every time the set was changed. The screens were made of light wooden frames and were fitted with grey transparent canvas and reversible hinges. Unfortunately they had a tendency to topple over and, on the first night in Moscow, it is said that they fell like dominoes! Nevertheless, Stanislavsky records that, 'The production of *Hamlet* met with great success. Some people were enthusiastic, others criticised, but everybody was excited, and debated, read reports, wrote articles, while other theatres in the country quietly appropriated the ideas of Craig, publishing them as their own' (Stanislavsky, 1945: 523).

Craig's ideas for set design were based on a philosophical concept rather than a particular interpretation of a play. He later admitted that the screens had been wrong for *Hamlet*. His son, Edward A. Craig, wrote, 'He realised that he should never have attempted to use his screens for the play at all - it was like trying to play a piece of music on an instrument for which it was not composed' (Arnott, 1975: 77). In this particular instance the mechanics of the set failed the design.

Despite this failure, Craig's influence was obvious. Similar scenic devices appeared in a production in 1913 by the Russian director Vladimir Mayakovsky. This was not a production of *Hamlet* but a tragedy called *Vladimir Mayakovsky*. In Russia the extent of Craig's influence was seen in productions of *Hamlet* across the country, in 1924 in Moscow and in 1925 in Tblisi. The 1925 production in Tblisi used screens but, unlike Craig, placed them on a revolving disc. Behind was the bleak shape of Elsinore and an enormous stairway which lead to the castle. It was on this stairway that the principle scenes took place. It aimed to symbolise 'all the life and movement of a man, his ups and downs' (Rudnitsky, 1988: 279).

For a production in Baku at the Azerbaidzhan State Theatre in 1926, the director, Alexander Tuganov, transferred the tragedy's action to an abstract Oriental country. He gave its characters (except Hamlet and Ophelia) Muslim names and designed the set in a style mid-way between Persian and Turkish. The Azerbaidzhani dramatist Dzhafar Dzhabarly, whose translation orientalised *Hamlet*, was convinced that he was guided by Goethe's view of 'the necessity of applying the works of Shakespeare to the conditions of a given stage'. In a letter to the director he expressed satisfaction that the play was played against an eastern background and that everything down to the minor detail was oriental. The critics agreed that there was little sense in presenting a Danish Elsinore as this would reduce its 'universal significance to nought' (Rudnitsky, 1988: 178-9).

These three productions all started from the same play and the same initial scenic inspiration but they were very different from one another. The scenic devices were used as a machine and gradually became more sophisticated and successful with new engineering.

The concept of the theatre set as an environment is perhaps the most modern in its theory and it has much to do with the rise of particular types of theatre building. During the 1960s and 1970s in Britain an attempt was made to take the theatre building closer to the idea of an Elizabethan stage. This is evident in the building of Chichester Festival Theatre in 1962, Sheffield Crucible Theatre in 1971, the Olivier Stage, as part of the Royal National Theatre in 1976, the Victoria Theatre, Stoke on Trent 1962, and the Manchester Royal Exchange Theatre built in 1976. The theatres at Chichester, Sheffield and London used an open thrust stage form, the Stoke and Manchester theatres were theatres-in-the-round. Several stages around the country with proscenium arches were modified and adapted to the new vogue. An example is the Royal Shakespeare Theatre at Stratford-on-Avon. Here the stage became the symbol of another separate world and the absence of set became a presence, a statement about the relationship between theatre and the world, the stage and the auditorium.

At the Royal Shakespeare Company Buzz Goodbody was trying to produce Shakespeare in a single environment. In 1975 she directed a much acclaimed production of *Hamlet* at the Other Place, the Royal Shakespeare Company's third theatre space in Stratford. Opened in 1974, the Other Place was originally an old tin hut and had been used as a store. Her policy was to only mount productions on a shoe string with total budgets ranging from between £50 and £150. For the *Hamlet* directed by Goodbody the set, designed by Chris Dyer, was minimal but the audience was included in the environment.

There was a raised shallow platform against white screens, ramps at the side and a kabuki-style bridge running through the audience to the rear. The screens served as an arras and clicked back and forth like a camera shutter for the entrances and exits. These overlapped like baton changers in a relay race. The sliding screens could form a continuous neutral coloured wall or, when on the rare occasions they were open, they could provide a central entrance or recess. An occasional table or stool gave the basis to the characters in particular situations - Polonius at his desk, Gertrude at her dressing table. The costumes were modern dress. Hamlet always kept the audience in view, sitting on the edge of the stage, talking to them as if to a confidant. The action took place all around and on Laertes's return to Elsinore he slammed the actual theatre doors, thus implying further that the whole space was Elsinore.

The Ghost first appeared at the back of the auditorium, spotlighted from the stage by the torches of the Danish police represented by Marcellus and Bernardo. The disappearance of the Ghost was executed equally effectively. During the exchange between Hamlet and the Ghost, Hamlet was at the back of the auditorium and the Ghost on stage. The audience turned their heads tennis match fashion as each spoke. After Hamlet's final speech to the Ghost, when the audience returned their gaze to the stage the Ghost had seemingly magically disappeared. For the dumbshow the players wore plain white masks (see fig. 5). The scene was spotlit by a Player in the central gangway. Polonius fell to his death dragging down the whole Arras/curtain. This simplified the disposal of the body, ready-wrapped as it were, at the end of the scene. The staging was simple but extremely effective. The setting for this production could be categorised as environmental in the sense that it happened all around. The audience was seated in an area which the actors also used as an additional playing space.

The role of the designer has gradually become more prominent over the last hundred years, particularly as a result of the work of Edward Gordon Craig. By the 1960s the role of the designer had become firmly consolidated and their involvement and influence on a production is now considered paramount. The director's closest aide in any theatrical presentation has come to be the designer. John Bury, a designer at the Royal Shakespeare Company in the 1960s, in interview stated that the function of the set in a Shakespeare production was twofold: it should be first 'a fluid framework that will not impede Shakespeare's swift changes in location and time, and second the correct symbol that will place in the mind of the audience the vital image of the play concerned' (Bury, 1966: 56).

Despite the somewhat schematic categorisation of the productions described above, it is rare that things are so clear cut, categories merge. How, one might ask, is it possible to differentiate between an environmental setting that symbolises a vital image and one which does not? Ultimately our categories matter little. Any further distinction of the images and concepts should be made in relation to the particular performance under the microscope.

Bob Crowley's design for the Barbican production of 1992 with Kenneth Branagh as *Hamlet* located the period of the production at the turn of the century. It had a look of Scandinavia and was reminiscent of the late nineteenth-century Norwegian dramatist, Henrik Ibsen. The Ghost made his first appearance emerging through the soil of a tiny untended cemetery located downstage which remained visible throughout the play. In this design we move from the formal columns of the court to Polonius's office stacked with floor-to-ceiling filing cabinets. Ophelia's bedroom was presented with painted nursery furniture. For the play within the play, the Players' acting area was right down stage, with dressing tables visible to the audience. When the Players performed they did so with their backs to the audience; they faced Claudius and members of the court who were seated in a replica theatre that filled the false proscenium with full scale seating (see fig. 6). The action opened out to the full stage depth for the transformation of Ophelia's nursery into a landscape of dead leaves and flowers before her suicide. This space later became the duelling ground for Hamlet and Laertes and the final moment when the Ghost received his son's corpse. The production was reviewed as offering up 'dozens of unforgettable images' (Herbert, 1993: 41)

Such visual and theatrical images may, however, be in competition with a play's linguistic imagery. The designer must always consider whether a design supports and brings new insights to a text or whether it detracts from its understanding.

The 1991 production of *Hamlet* by the touring theatre company Cheek By Jowl brings us full cycle - to a utilitarian approach. There was a put-up stage in the shape of a platform. This had a curtain which was attached by the actors for the Players' scene. It also represented the battlements, the court, and, when covered with a red bedspread, Gertrude's bed. Above, a canopy was moved on pulleys to create different spaces for different scenes. There was a stage cloth hanging upstage as a backing to the whole of the stage and for the Queen's closet. Another cloth was added for the arras. All the changes in the setting were carried out by the actors. The staging was simple and the platform stage gave the production a specific sense of its own space, irrespective of the architectural arrangements of the theatres it played in. It also located the performance symbolically as the actors, on entering, stood on the platform to suggest they were actors about to embark on the telling of the tale of Hamlet. The design moved swiftly and the canopies had the effect of sweeping the next scene on stage. The set itself was reminiscent of the resources used by Elizabethan touring actor troupes who would put up a stage and perform in the innyards. This style of presentation is, now as then, most suitable for touring. It claims the space in whatever performance venue.

A third Globe Theatre is currently being built on the south bank of the Thames (see fig. 7). The dimensions of the original Globe have been discovered and archaeological digs have provided enough information to build a replica of Shakespeare's theatre. Notwithstanding, the question of how to stage a Shakespeare play is still perplexing. Panels of designers and academics are arguing over, for instance, the width of the doors at the back of the stage. In addition to the archaeological evidence they also have to take into consideration modern staging requirements, as the building is to be used as a performance space, not as a museum. On the one hand, the designers want the entrances to be high enough to allow actors to enter carrying banners and spears, so that they can be back-lit and shrouded in smoke. On the other hand, the academics argue that this would make the dimensions incompatible with those of Shakespeare's Globe.

Whatever the final design of the third Globe it will be a crucial factor in forming the image we have of the potentialities and actualities of Elizabethan staging. More importantly, perhaps, it will enrich the imaginative and creative possibilities of staging Shakespeare's and other dramatists' work.

Shakespeare's 'Text' of *Hamlet*

ROBIN HAMILTON

Pol.   What do you read, my lord?
Ham. Words, words, words.
(2.2.191-2)

Yes, but are they Shakespeare's?

Shakespeare was born in 1564 and probably began his writing career in his early twenties sometime in the 1580s. He continued writing plays until about 1612, when he retired to Stratford where he died four years later in 1616. In 1623, seven years after his death, his thirty-six 'collected plays' were published by his fellow actors John Heminges and Henry Condell in what is now known as the Folio.

The Folio was a large, expensive and enormously successful work. Between its original publication in 1623, and 1685, three further editions of it were printed. However, during Shakespeare's actual writing career, between 1594 and 1615, eighteen of his plays had already been published in Quarto. (Of these eighteen plays, *Pericles*, published in Quarto in 1609, is the only one not to be included in the Folio). Unlike the Folio, these Quartos were small, cheap editions of single plays.

That only half of Shakespeare's plays were published during his life is not, given the circumstances of the time, surprising. What is more surprising, indeed, is that as many as half of them were published during his theatrical career. The reason for this is that the absence of copyright laws meant that no theatre company held a specific monopoly in producing and acting a particular play. If a play had been licensed, anyone who could get hold of a copy was at liberty to stage it. As a result, the only way which a theatre company could keep control of a play was to prevent anyone else getting a copy of it.

The reasons why plays would nevertheless be published by the companies which owned them were various - an unauthorised edition (see below on the Bad Quartos) might somehow have appeared, making the retention of the original less important (as was the case with *Hamlet*); the company might urgently be in need of money, and be willing to abandon attempts to protect a play for the immediate return to be gained by selling a copy to a bookseller. In England at that time, unlike today, it was the actual bookseller who would sell the physical copy of a book who was responsible for publishing it. A further reason why a Quarto might be issued is that a company might have become so closely associated with a particular play that it would not matter if copies were generally available. It is due to these reasons, or perhaps more than one in combination, that so many of Shakespeare's plays were issued during his lifetime. It should be stressed that, while it would not usually be worth publishing an unpopular play, the fact that a play was not published in Quarto did not by itself mean that it was unpopular. It might simply be the case that the theatre company would profit more by retaining the exclusive control of the manuscript. For example, because *The Tempest* did not appear in print until the Folio of 1623, nearly ten years after it was written does not mean that it was an unpopular play.

Quartos came in two kinds - Good Quartos and Bad Quartos. The good Quartos would be, finally, issued by the acting company which owned the play. Bad Quartos, on the other hand, would be the result of theft, deception, or intrigue. Someone might, for instance, attend a performance of the play, and either take notes at the time (if he could get away with it) or write down what he remembered immediately afterwards. Some of the minor actors in the play might be bribed to recite their own parts as well as all they could remember of the speeches of the other actors. The result of this is often a published version of the play which (not unexpectedly) often bears little resemblance to the original. The point is emphatically made by the Bad Quarto version of part of what is probably the play's most famous speech:

> To be, or not to be, I there's the point,
> To Die, to sleepe, is that all? I all:
> No, to sleepe, to dreame, I mary there it goes,
> For in that dreame of death, when wee awake,

And borne before an euerlasting Iudge,
From whence no passenger euer retur'nd,
The vndiscoured country, at whose sight
The happy smile, and the accursed damn'd.

(Spencer, 1980: 362)

In many ways, the nature of a Good Quarto depends on the point at which it was extracted from the evolution of the play. The earliest stage of a play by Shakespeare is what is known as the Foul Papers. These would be the original manuscript which Shakespeare would submit to the theatre company, called the Foul Papers because they might be overwritten by Shakespeare when he added in corrections over the first draft of the text. They might also be inconsistent, and would probably be lacking in stage-directions. Based on this, the company would produce a Prompt Copy - a copy of the play written out by a professional scribe, with the names of the characters made consistent (Shakespeare himself sometimes forgot the names he had given to minor characters!) and with the stage directions written in. This version would be used (which is where the name comes from) to prompt the actors when they forgot their lines. Later, in the course of rehearsal or production, the company might make changes to the play based on what did or didn't work when it was actually performed. On the whole, however, Good Quartos derive either from Shakespeare's manuscript original: the Foul Papers - or from the tidy version of this produced for the company: the Prompt Copy.

When the Folio was put together, eighteen of the thirty-six plays contained in it were published there for the first time. Of the remaining eighteen plays, some were taken directly from an earlier published Quarto text; some were based on the Quarto with revisions and emendations from some other source; and in some cases, however, the Quarto and Folio versions of the plays differ quite considerably.

For a long time, it was assumed that where there was a difference between the Quarto and Folio texts, this was because they each partly represented a lost 'original' by Shakespeare, and the way to recover this better text of the play was to put together all the bits which could be found in either the Quarto or the Folio, to produce what is now called a composite text. More recently (and more reasonably) considered opinion is that where there are differences between the

Quarto and the Folio texts, this probably represents changes and revisions made by either Shakespeare himself or the acting company in the course of rehearsing or performing the play. In these terms, as a rough rule-of-thumb, the Quartos will tend to represent Shakespeare's original version of a play, and the Folio will more likely represent the stage the play had reached when it had settled down after revisions made during rehearsal and performance.

What does all this have to do with *Hamlet*? Well, first of all, versions of *Hamlet* exist in all three forms - there is a Bad Quarto (1603); a Good Quarto (1604); and the Folio (1623). Until recently, most texts of *Hamlet* were constructed by taking the Good Quarto and adding to it all the bits in the Folio not found in the Good Quarto itself. However, in the recent collected edition of Shakespeare's plays, published by Oxford University Press in 1988, what we are given is the version of the text as it's found in the Folio, with the extra bits from the Quarto published as an Appendix. This version gives us a Hamlet who has, for instance, fewer soliloquies than we usually find him speaking.

In terms of the editions with which most students will work, the following lines and scenes are present in the Quarto and not the Folio (references are to the line numbers in the Alexander (1951) edition of Shakespeare's plays):

1.1.108 I think it be no other but e'n so... Unto our climatures and countrymen (125)

1.4.17 They clepe us drunkards, and with swinish phrase... To his own scandal (38)

1.4.75 The very place puts toys of desperation... And hears it roar beneath (78)

3.2.166-7 Where love is great, the littlest doubts are fear; / Where little fears grow great, great love grows there

3.2.312-4 To desperation turn my trust and hope, / An anchor's cheer in prison be my scope

3.3.71 Sense, sure, you have... Could not so mope (81)
[Of this speech, the Folio retains: 'What devil was't / That thus hath cozen'd you at hoodman-blind? ']

3.4.161 That monster custom, who all sense doth eat... With wondrous potency (170)

[Of this speech, the Folio retains: 'Refrain tonight; / And that shall lend a kind of easiness / To the next abstinence ']

3.4.202 There's letters seal'd; and my two school-fellows... When in one line two crafts directly meet (210)

4.1.40 so haply slander... And hit the woundless air (44)

4.4.7 I will do't, my lord... My thoughts be bloody, or be nothing worth! (66)

4.7.68 My lord, I will be rul'd... Importing health and graveness (81)

4.7.100 The scrimers of their nation... If you oppos'd them (102)

4.7.114 There lives within the very flame of love... That hurts by easing. But to the quick of th'ulcer (123)

5.2.106 here is newly come to court Laertes... in his meed he's unfellowed (140)

[In place of this, the Folio has: 'you are not ignorant of what excellence Laertes is at his weapon'

5.2.152-3 I knew you must be edified by the margent ere you had done

5.2.189 *Enter a* LORD... She well instructs me (200)

If you mark these scenes for deletion in your own text of *Hamlet*, you'll probably have a copy which will be a better approximation to the text which was actually staged in 1601 than the one which is given to you for study.

How much does it matter if we make these changes? The play moves faster, and Hamlet himself has fewer soliloquies than in the text with which we are familiar. It is worth noting that the first time that we find people talking of Hamlet delaying is after the composite text, conflating the Quarto and Folio, is put together in the eighteenth century. Our Hamlet may delay, but maybe it's the case that Shakespeare's Hamlet doesn't!

A Note on Materials:

Perhaps the best short discussion of the problems - and the productive relations - of Quarto and Folio texts is:

Jonathan Bate (1991), 'Shakespeare's Tragedies as working scripts'.

Good general descriptions of the nature of Quarto and Folio texts, and discussions of particular plays can be found in:

F.E. Halliday (1964), *A Shakespeare Companion: 1564-1964*

Finally, however, the ultimate source of detail in this area is:

Stanley Wells and Gary Taylor (1987), *William Shakespeare: A Textual Companion*

For the modern sense of what Shakespeare's text is, see:
Stanley Wells and Gary Taylor (1988), *The Complete Works.*
(As well as providing the Folio *Hamlet,* this edition prints two separate texts of *King Lear.*)

Based on the above text is the *Norton Shakespeare* edited by Stephen Greenblatt and others (1997) who make significant editorial changes.

Works Cited

Editions of Shakespeare's works

Alexander, Peter (1951), *The Complete Works* (London: Collins).

Theobald, Lewis (1740), *The Works of Shakespeare* (London: Lintott, Hitch, etc.).

Greenblatt, Stephan, *et al* (1997), *The Norton Shakespeare* (New York: Norton).

Wells, Stanley and Gary Taylor (1988), *The Complete Works* (Oxford: Oxford University Press).

Editions of *Hamlet*

Dover Wilson, J. (1934), [The New Cambridge Shakespeare] (Cambridge: Cambridge University Press).

Edwards, Philip (1985), [The New Cambridge Shakespeare] (Cambridge: Cambridge University Press).

Jenkins, Harold (1982), [The Arden Shakespeare] (London: Methuen).

Spencer, T.J.B. (1980), [The New Penguin Shakespeare] (Harmondsworth, Middlesex: Penguin).

Other works

Arnott, Brian (1975), *Towards A New Theatre: Edward Gordon Craig and Hamlet* (Ottawa: National Gallery of Canada).

Bablet, Denis (1981), *Edward Gordon Craig*, translated by Daphne Woodward (London: Methuen).

Jonathan Bate (1991), 'Shakespeare's Tragedies as working scripts', *Critical Survey* 3, 118-127.

Belsey, Catherine (1991), *The Subject of Tragedy*, second edition (London: Methuen).

Bowers, Fredson (1940), *Elizabethan Revenge Tragedy* (Princeton: Princeton University Press).

Bullough, Geoffrey, ed. (1957-73), *Narrative and Dramatic Sources of Shakespeare*, 7 vols (London: Routledge and Kegan Paul).

Bury, John (1966), 'John Bury Talking to Peter Roberts', *Plays and Players*, 13, No. 12 (September), 56.

Castiglione (1974), *The Book of the Courtier*, translated by Sir Thomas Hoby (London:Dent).

Cawley, A.C., ed. (1957), *'Everyman' and Medieval Miracle Plays*, second edition (London: Dent).

Dover Wilson, J. (1935), *What Happens in 'Hamlet'* (Cambridge: Cambridge University Press).

French, Marilyn (1982), *Shakespeare's Division of Experience* (London: Jonathon Cape).

Halliday, F.E. (1964), *A Shakespeare Companion: 1564-1964* (Harmondsworth, Middlesex: Penguin).

Herbert, Ian (1993), 'Two by Crowley', *Theatre Crafts International*, (April), 41.

Holderness, Graham (1988), *The Shakespeare Myth* (Manchester: Manchester University Press).

Machiavelli, Niccolò (1961), *The Prince*, translated by George Bull (Harmondsworth, Middlesex: Penguin).

Orrell, John (1988), *The Human Stage: English Theatre Design 1567-1640* (Cambridge: Cambridge University Press).

Rudnitsky, Konstantin (1988), *Russian and Soviet Theatre: Tradition and the Avant Garde*, translated by Roxane Permar, edited by Lesley Milne (London: Thames and Hudson).

Stanislavsky, Constantin (1945), *My Life In Art*, translated by J.J. Robbins, fourth edition (London: Bles).

Stoppard, Tom (1967), *Rosencrantz and Guildenstern Are Dead* (London: Faber).

Wallis, Mick (1991), 'Emblem, psychology and feeling: playing and reading *King Lear*', *Critical Survey* 3, 229-39.

Wells, Stanley and Gary Taylor (1987), *William Shakespeare: A Textual Companion* (Oxford: Oxford University Press).

Williams, Raymond (1968), *Drama from Ibsen to Brecht* (Harmondsworth, Middlesex: Penguin).